ATTACK ATTACK

THE STORY OF WEST BROMWICH ALBION
1978-79

BRITESPOT
PUBLISHING

This book is dedicated to
my mom and dad, the best anyone could have.

ATTACK ATTACK

A Britespot Publication

First Published in Great Britain by
Britespot Publishing Solutions Limited
Chester Road, Cradley Heath, West Midlands B64 6AB

© Dave Bowler 2004
© Britespot May 2004

ISBN 1 904103 31 6

Cover design and layout
© Britespot Publishing Solutions Limited

Printed and bound in the UK by Cromwell Press Limited

Dave Bowler Acknowledgments:
Many of the men from the 1978/79 side and beyond have given their time and memories to this book, so my thanks go out to Tony Brown, Cyrille Regis, John Wile, Willie Johnston, Brendon Batson, Ron Atkinson, Johnny Giles, Bryan Robson, Ally Brown, Bobby Hope, Don Howe and John Trewick. To them, and all the others who contributed to the Albion cause, this book pays tribute.

Thanks to everybody in the media office for their help with the book, notably Scott Field, John Simpson, Oliver Bhurrut and Mike Philpotts and to Stuart Curtis.

Thanks too to the legendary photographer Laurie Rampling, who can do things with a lens that you just wouldn't believe.

Most of all, thanks to Lisa for continuing to put up with football's demands, and to Sophie and Jonathan who probably enjoy them.

From Britespot Publishing: Paul Burns, Chris Russell, Gemma Davison and Lisa Winstanley.

Photos © West Bromwich Albion, Laurie Rampling, Graham Silk.

CONTENTS

INTRODUCTION

THE BEAUTIFUL & THE DAMNED

The great American film maker John Ford famously believed that, when you're confronted with a choice between truth and legend, you always print the legend. And as any event recedes further into the past, myth-making becomes more seductive still, embellishing for the sake of honouring the "good old days" – FA Cup winning captain Graham Williams once warned of that you should be wary of retired footballers discussing their exploits because, "the older we get, the better we were!"

True though that may be, it's equally foolhardy to dismiss the folklore that surrounds the past as nothing more than what Shakespeare called a "tale told by an idiot, full of sound and fury, signifying nothing." For there are times when legend and reality meet, when the tales are no taller than the achievements, which makes it all the more important that those days are captured while they're still comparatively recent, before they slip from memory into obscurity. Before we forget the who, the how, the why.

It was fitting that, in the year of Albion's centenary, 1978/79, the team should play the kind of rapturous, no-holds-barred attacking football that encapsulated the Baggies blend, our way of doing things in those first 100 years. West Bromwich Albion was long a club revered for its devotion to open, attacking football, to dashing wing play, enthralling centre forwards, for its willingness to entertain at all costs. And for all that the 1919/20 League Championship side had blazed 104 goals on its way to the title; for all that WG Richardson had turned goalscoring into an art in the 1930s; for all that Albion's 1953/54 side was as complete as any side that ever set foot on a field; and for all that the Astle-led 1960s team were the cup-fighting side par excellence, it was the school of 1978/79 that even now captures popular imagination both in Baggie ranks and beyond.

7

In part that's because they played in the age of colour TV, when video killed the radio star- an advantage which eluded the likes of Jesse Pennington- while even film depicting Allen and Barlow is in short supply, and most of the exploits of Astle and Hope are only captured in flickering black and white. But Ron Atkinson's side were caught and preserved in glorious technicolour, not least their crowning moment, the 5-3 win over Manchester United in their theatre of dreams: an almost perfect exposition of attacking football saved for posterity by the Star Soccer cameras and now available on DVD.

That hour or so of film tells you everything about the way that side went about their football, the swagger in their step, their self-belief and their never-wavering determination to drive forward, to keep on playing, attacking, taking the game to the opposition. Yet that doesn't tell the rest of the story, the beauty of the side, the political statement of playing three great black footballers in the Britain of 1978, the aesthetic beauty of that particular navy-blue-and-white shirt or those luminous yellow and green stripes and, overwhelmingly, the all-too-human frailty of the team, the vulnerability: a side always teetering on the brink. Albion were David Bowie, damaged by daring, sometimes bloodied but always beautiful.

Some argue that the fact that they never carried off the title or a cup means that, ultimately, they were a failure. But history might suggest the very opposite, that they didn't collect any silverware makes them more endearing, more memorable, more loveable perhaps: beautiful losers.

And that side is loved by those of us who were there and even by those younger supporters who have never seen an Albion shirt without a sponsor's logo emblazoned upon it. Scott Fitzgerald once wrote of "The Beautiful and The Damned" and that, in a sense, was the story of that season: a side that had so much that the fates couldn't then bestow medals and trophies. It shone so hard then crashed and burned, disintegrating in a matter of months, taking the club with it for nearly twenty years, as if no one place, certainly not such a parochial town as West Bromwich, could contain so much talent, so much energy, so many ideas, as if it were destined to blow itself apart. This was a team and a season that had everything.

Print the legend? There's no need. The truth's good enough.

CHAPTER ONE

WHERE DID IT ALL GO RIGHT?

May 18th 1979. A Friday night at The Hawthorns, a rarity in itself in the days before Rupert Murdoch reorganised the fixture list for the benefit of those watching in Tokyo and Toronto.

Albion needed only to avoid defeat against Nottingham Forest to claim the runners-up slot in Division One for the first time since the near-double-winning season of 1953/54, 25 years earlier. After a season when the Baggies had illuminated English – and European – football with a swashbuckling brand of the game based on entertaining, on playing the game the right way no matter what the consequences might be, on attack, attack, second place was our last hope of tangible reward. Liverpool and the elements had conspired to rob us of the title, European cynicism put the UEFA Cup beyond us, but second place in the league was still a huge achievement for a side which three and a half years earlier had been struggling in the lower reaches of Division Two.

Ten minutes to go, and Albion and Forest were locked at 0-0, with Forest having more than half an eye on the European Cup Final less than a fortnight later, a meeting with Malmo that would give Brian Clough his crowning moment of glory. Surely we wouldn't fall at the final hurdle now?

Of course, we did. That was what Albion were about, beauty, glory, but ultimately, frailty. It was that very fragility that made them so special, put them above the common herd. You could admire Liverpool or Forest, but you loved Albion- even people who weren't Baggies fans. That side had all the attributes of the great icons of the rock'n'roll age, we were football's James Dean, Marilyn Monroe, Ziggy Stardust. We were glamorous, we were beautiful, we were thrilling, we lived fast and we died young, much too young, before that team could achieve all it should have, but before it could be rendered ugly by decay, so that even now it burns bright in the hearts and minds of those who lived with it, who had the joy of watching it week after week for one glorious, unforgettable season.

9

I remember watching the game unfold from the Smethwick End and being crushed when Trevor Francis popped up to steal that late winner in front of the Birmingham Road End. I remember turning to my dad, a veteran of the 1954 season, and asking him if that was really it, if it was all over. As dads do, if you're lucky enough to have a good one, he turned things on their head and made me feel ok about it – "They'll be back. We'll be better next season."

How were any of us to know that we wouldn't get better, that we'd peaked? How were we to know that within a couple of weeks the heart would be ripped out of the side with the departure of Laurie Cunningham and Len Cantello: the silk and the steel? How were we to know that the party was over?

Sadly, it was a team fated to fail, if trophies are your only measure of success. But for those of us who were there, that season was nothing but a triumph, a high watermark in our appreciation of the Albion, of football. Ron Atkinson, manager of that great side, says now that, "I've watched Arsenal this year, the way they put Celta Vigo out of Europe and Portsmouth out of the FA Cup, and they are the nearest I've seen to that Albion side. The way they attack, their pace and movement. That's how good we were that year."

But something always conspired to ensure we didn't get above ourselves, that we were always taken down a peg or two, kicked back to our dour Black Country origins. Even when we broke the transfer record with the signing of David Mills from Middlesbrough for an incomprehensible £516,000, it still all went horribly wrong. Not only did Mills turn out to be a disastrous buy for the club, but our record was trumped within weeks when Cloughie made Trevor Francis the first ever million-pound footballer, all but doubling our suddenly meagre-looking outlay. And who popped up to steal second place from us on the last day of the season? Trevor Francis. Summed it up really.

Like all overnight successes, it was years in the making, the irony being that a team lauded for its verve, its invention and its vitality had its roots in defence, in organisation and, most of all, in failure.

To find the genesis of Albion's 1978/79 side, you have to go back to the summer of 1971 when the Baggies board made a huge statement of ambition, FA Cup winning manager Alan Ashman being the first casualty. Bobby Hope, creative lynchpin of the great cup-winning team of the 1960s, remembers that, for chairman Jim Gaunt, only one trophy mattered. "We'd won the FA Cup and the League Cup, played in a couple of finals and semi finals, so it was a successful period for the club. But after we'd lost the League Cup Final to Manchester City in 1970, he came in and said, "These cups are well and good, but it's time we won the league." That was the beginning of the end and Alan Ashman went – sacked while he was on holiday a year later."

With Ashman went Albion's trademark passing game, meaning the end of the road for Hope: no fan of the style that Ashman's successor, Don Howe, tried to introduce. "Don had coached the Arsenal team that won the double in 1971, so you couldn't argue with his track record, and of course, he'd played here for years before that. But he just wanted me to run up and down all the time, not to get on the ball. That was no good for me. I had to get on the ball, that was my game. You can get anybody off the street to run up and down, but you need footballers to win you games."

Howe's arrival either coincided with or caused Albion's demise, depending on your viewpoint. His first season saw the Baggies remain in lower mid-table while going out of both cup competitions at the first hurdle as Howe tried to change things around- too quickly according to one of his first signings, Alistair Brown, who joined from Leicester. "I think where Don Howe went wrong was he tried to get a lot of young lads in the team at once, tried to finish a few players off before they were ready maybe, like Bobby Hope. And it never worked because it's hard to replace players that good with kids." In his defence, Howe argued, "We weren't blessed with money so I tried to find youngsters, players on the way up, because in the main, this club couldn't buy established stars. But that's always a long-term thing because you have to bring them on, the same as a youth policy almost."

The Baggies tumbled out of Division One in 1972/73, an ignominious bottom of the table, four points from safety and for the next two seasons, they toiled badly in an effort to find salvation and promotion, as Tony Brown remembers. "To be honest, the only way you could see us getting out of Division Two was by going into Division Three!" Like all the strikers, Bomber struggled under Don Howe's disciplines which were all about getting men behind the ball, closing down, tackling back, being solid. Ally Brown found that especially difficult to get to grips with. "Holding the ball up was never my strength, I never enjoyed having my back to goal, I liked things in front of me, but Don used to work with me for ages at getting better with my back to goal, and in fact he used to try to get me to put weight on, telling me to drink Guinness. I think he wanted to make me another Ray Kennedy who'd been a target man for him at Arsenal before he dropped into midfield at Liverpool. Ray was a big 14-stone lad and I was probably 11 and a half!"

Tony Brown found things even tougher as one of the few survivors of the glory days of the 1960s. "Don had his opinions and that was it. He wouldn't listen to you. It was the lowest time of my career and I very nearly left for Crystal Palace because I wasn't enjoying coming into work in a morning." Albion's captain, John Wile, expands on Bomber's troubles. "Don came in and said, "I'm going to make you a better player than what you are." That's where Don's man management was poor, because he didn't mean it as critically as it sounded, but as a player, it got your back up. Tony was a very good player, played for England, so I don't think he took kindly to that! We used to room together and I always said to him, "Do the tracking back, help out when you can, but don't forget your strength is scoring goals. While you're scoring goals, you'll never be out the team." But Tony was such an honest lad that he concentrated so much on doing what Don Howe asked him that he lost his edge going forward; he stopped scoring goals and ended up out of the side."

Wile and his central defensive colleague Alistair Robertson were two of the new players that Don Howe had introduced to the side as regulars and they, probably more than anyone, benefited from his four-year tenure at The Hawthorns, as Wile points out. "Don has taken a lot of criticism, unfairly at times, because the results didn't show the work that he put in and the legacy he left. He did a huge amount of work on the defensive things, which didn't bear fruit in his time. I think a fair criticism of him would be to say he was an excellent coach but his man management skills let him down. But in terms of getting our organisation right at the back, he was spot on and that was what a lot of our later success was built on. It was just that, with the players we had under Ron Atkinson, people only noticed that the front players were exciting! But the defensive disciplines were our foundation."

11

After a couple of seasons of Second Division mediocrity, Don Howe's number was up and the Albion board decided that, once again, it was time for a change, a decision Howe now looks back on philosophically. "I worked harder during that period than anywhere. I worked my socks off, put everything into it, but I couldn't get results to save my life. But I think the work I did was ultimately fruitful, some good came from it for the club. When I left, I felt it was ok; everybody was doing their job properly, players were training right, we had good pros, it was in good shape. I felt I was just missing one piece in the team." In fairness to Howe, he had identified who that player was, but he just couldn't get hold of him. "If I could have got John Giles as a player, I think we would have gone up. Having him in the middle was the difference between my team and his."

Ironically, weeks after Howe was shown the door in the dog days of the 1974/75 season, Giles was appointed Albion's first ever player manager, and for Tony Brown, it was a change that couldn't come a moment too soon. "He was the most important signing we'd made in years. John put us on the right road and he deserves a lot more credit than he sometimes gets because he was definitely the instigator of it all. He changed the place round, got us buzzing again, got the players enjoying the game again."

In spite of that, in spite of his immaculate pedigree having worked under Sir Matt Busby and Don Revie, it took a while for Giles to turn things around, as John Wile remembers. "It took a while for John to decide to take the job on properly. When he first came, the job was fresh and he didn't grasp the nettle; he left Brian Whitehouse to do the coaching, nothing much changed and results were poor. The only time I was ever dropped at Albion was by John, and he was right because I wasn't playing well. I said to him, "Fair enough, but why don't you leave yourself out, because you're not playing well either!" And he said, "No, I'm not. But I'm the manager and I pick the team!" Admitting to himself that he picked the team seemed to be a big thing because, from that day on, he took charge. We hardly saw Brian; John ran the first team, brought in his own training methods, a lot of short, small-sided games with a premium put on doing it right. The habits you got into in the week were to be carried into the game – passing it accurately, closing down, tracking back, not losing possession.

"John Giles wasn't in the same league as Don as a coach, but he got far more out of the players in performances and results, because he was a terrific manager of people. Being a manager isn't just about passing an exam, there's much more to it than that. John came in at the right time; we had good youngsters coming through, we were well organised at the back and we just needed somebody in the middle to pull it together. Adding John as a player was the big step forward. The term "world class" is over used, but not in John's case. Having him in the team made it better straightaway, and he then made the rest of us better players simply by being around him. People like myself and Alistair Robertson, who were seen as rough-and-ready before then, suddenly developed, not least because John was always available for the ball when you had it.

"He used to say to us, "You can tackle, win the ball, that's your strength. I can pass it, that's mine. You win it and then give it to me. Then we're all doing what we're good at, we'll play from there." And because of that, my own game developed. I'd get it, give him a pass, nice and easy. Because you did that, you tended to make an angle because you weren't frightened to get it back, and you became involved in a move two or three times rather than just winning it and getting rid of it. Confidence grows and once we got going, we were on our way. Once that started, you wouldn't have swapped our players for anybody else in the country because we thought that much about each other."

Results were poor initially as Giles admits. "We got off to a poor start, and I think the problems were mostly my fault, I made too many changes early on, but once we settled we became a very good side very quickly, which was no surprise as we had a lot of good players." Ally Brown was one of them, and he enjoyed a new lease of life under the Irishman. "He was good for me; it was nice to have a manager that picked me regularly, and he got us playing some good stuff. It was all possession; he always said the biggest crime was giving the ball away. As a striker it could be frustrating because you'd make half a dozen runs before the ball would come, but it worked because he got us up straight away. He said I was a similar player to Mick Jones up at Leeds, and I could see that."

Ally's namesake Tony remains a fully-paid-up member of the Johnny Giles fan club, noting, "Even when it went poorly to start with, there was no panic. We were down the bottom at Christmas, but he'd say, "Don't worry. I'll carry the can, I'll take the criticism. We're going to play this way and results will turn. I believe in what we're doing, things will change." And it clicked in the new year, we went on a phenomenal run of form, and by the last game, we knew that a win at Oldham would send us back up. I got the only goal, one of the most important I ever scored. Paddy Mulligan knocked in a cross, Ally Brown nodded it down to me on the edge of the box and I ficked it up in the air with my right foot and volleyed it in with my left. It flew in and we were up."

Promotion brought problems though as Giles looked set to turn his back on the club. "I never liked management to be honest and I told the players I was thinking of resigning. But they wanted me to stick with it, and in the end I carried on because I didn't think I could leave the club in the lurch just before its first season back in Division One."

Fortunately Giles did reconsider and took Albion into their first season back in the top flight, for although the gap between the top two divisions was nowhere near as yawning as it is today, a return to football's top table was still daunting for any side. Unlike the Leeds of today however, when Albion's lengthy stay in the top flight ended, it hadn't been the signal for a mass exodus and the promoted side was chock full of top-class players with huge experience such as Osborne, Bomber Brown, Johnston and Cantello, while judicious additions had been made in the shape of Mick Martin, Paddy Mulligan and Giles himself. On top of that, probably the greatest player Albion ever produced was making his presence felt – Bryan Robson. The emergence of Robson underlined just what a great breeding-ground for talent The Hawthorns was.

"I came through the ranks with a few others, the likes of John Trewick and Derek Statham, and just like Manchester United have shown, that does help because it takes the pressure off individuals. You learn together, you make progress together, and that helps give you a good team spirit as well. It was good for me because Albion were always strong when it came to scouting in the North east and in Scotland, they found the likes of Bobby Hope and Ally Robertson in the past, myself and John Trewick, so the system worked well. When you can come through the ranks, it gives you a special feel for a club. You feel a part of it and that just increases your determination to succeed there.

"It wasn't plain sailing because, just as I was breaking through in Johnny's team, I did have a lot of trouble with injury. I broke my leg three times in a short space of time, but I never really worried about it finishing my career. In a funny way, it stood me in good stead in that you half feel that your career might suffer, it might go away from you, but once you get over the injuries, it makes you more determined to have a career in football, and it helps you deal with any injuries you do get later on."

Albion were presented with a tough start to the campaign, a trip to Giles' old home, Elland Road. "It was a red-hot day, we were 2-0 up, should have won, but there was a lack of confidence and we ended up drawing 2-2. It was a matter of getting into the habit of winning. But it was a growing team and we had some terrific wins. We were playing terrible at home to Spurs, 2-0 down at the break, and then came back and beat them 4-2. Then the next home game was Manchester United, and we thumped them 4-0. They're still great memories."

Albion went on to finish seventh, just shy of a UEFA Cup slot, but with the season over, Giles decided this time it really was the end. "It was a very tough decision because the place was on the move, we could only get better, but management wasn't for me. If I had my time again, I probably wouldn't have left because I had two of the happiest years of my life at The Hawthorns. I can't speak too highly of the fans, the players, everyone at the club."

Again, the players were shattered by the decision, though it was something they'd expected this time round, as John Wile says. "It was sad when he left. He said he'd been earning more when we were in the Second Division than in the First because he'd got a promotion bonus, we were getting more

13

win bonuses in the lower division to start with, and he felt that was wrong, which of course it was. And John stood by his principles, and when the directors were slow in coming forward with a new offer, it upset him and he wouldn't put up with it. We all pleaded with him not to go but his mind was made up.

"The big question then was who would replace him. Ronnie Allen always was destined to come back as manager I suppose, and without being disrespectful, when clubs lose a manager, the replacement is often someone who is handy, and Ronnie was in the right place at the right time. He was idolised at West Brom, a good track record abroad and he was a good appointment. He saw he'd got a good team and he had the savvy not to interfere with anything; he kept it bubbling along. We had the right attitude which Don had started and John had really instilled, that nobody was bigger than anybody else, the team was the most important thing, sometimes you had to sacrifice your game for the good of the team. That was ingrained. A lot of managers want to come in and make changes just to have an impact, but he was brave enough not to."

Allen had been back at The Hawthorns since the start of 1977 in a consultancy role, perhaps a recognition by the board that Giles' tenure was always destined to be temporary. It was a masterstroke as it turned out, for Allen was instrumental in two of Giles' key signings that would transform the club, not just on the field, but as an institution. Laurie Cunningham was plucked from Orient's side for just £110,000, Joe Mayo heading in the opposite direction as part of the deal. Cunningham made his debut at White Hart Lane in a 2-0 win, then made his Hawthorns bow in an unforgettable night under the lights on March 16th 1977. A quarter of a century on, it's hard to imagine just how extraordinary it was to see a black player in an Albion kit, but Laurie and his generation were real trailblazers. Over the course of 90 minutes, Cunningham had the crowd eating out of his hand, matching the dazzling skills and pace of crowd-favourite Willie Johnston, scoring a goal and playing a huge part in the 4-0 demolition of Ipswich, Bryan Robson getting the other three. Cunningham was electrifying and with six goals in 13 games, he heralded the next phase of Albion's development.

Yet Allen's greatest feat of talent spotting was still to come, discovering a new centre forward playing in the Isthmian League on the outskirts of London. Cyrille Regis was playing for Hayes and recalls that "Ronnie Allen had heard about this big, raw black guy and came to see me play. He used to tell the story that he saw me go up for a ball and put it in the net along with four defenders and decided there and then that I'd do! He had to persuade the board to buy me, even threatening to pay for me himself. I had a one-year deal, the club paid Hayes £10,000 altogether after so many games for Albion, and they bought the floodlights with the money – they're still there now!"

Regis had barely signed his contract before Giles was off and Allen installed in his place. "I didn't start work here until the pre-season in 1977/78, and by then Johnny Giles had left and Ronnie had taken over as manager, which was a massive help because he obviously believed in me. But the training! I'd trained twice a week in the past, but suddenly it was every day, twice a day in pre-season, and I was absolutely wrecked. And I was away from London, didn't know anybody, so it was tough to settle, but I was lucky that I got in the first team nearly straight away because of injuries and that set me off."

14

History shows that Regis quickly burst into the team, Tony Brown recalling his impact. "Once he got into full-time training, his pace and strength shone through, got in for a League Cup game and then played in the First Division against Middlesbrough. I remember it well because I was injured, and I watched it from the stand, and he scored that unbelievable goal where he got it on the halfway line, turned, and just ran with it. Nobody scored goals like that, and that was Cyrille started, and after that it was all just one way for him."

The Brummie Road had been desperate for someone to succeed The King, and Cyrille was the man, his emergence part of an exciting start to the season that saw Allen encouraging Albion to be a bit more attack-minded. The Baggies were up with the division hotshots, but again, change was in the air as Wile recalls. "Ronnie got an offer to go to Saudi and he asked me for advice, and all I said was to get down to Smith's and buy a box of pens just in case the first one ran out when he was signing the contract! You didn't get offers like that, something like £100,000, back in 1978, unbelievable money; nobody could turn that down. Myself and George Wright kept things going until Ron Atkinson arrived in January, which again was the right appointment at the right time. He was what we'd never had, a big, loud, brash figure. He gave us that bit of glamour and took the club onto the next level."

Looking back on his arrival in January 1978, Atkinson says, "It was probably the only time I've ever taken over a side that was doing ok! Johnny Giles had set things up, and when I got here we had a good side, though I felt it had just started to go off the boil a little bit. But the attitude was good, confidence was high. Under Johnny, they'd been very much a side that passed the ball, complete possession, very patient, and I had no problems with that. But I felt that, looking at the front players we had, they were so quick, if we just speeded up our attacking play a little bit, it would be beneficial to them. But it was only a slight adjustment, just a tweak really."

The highlight of Atkinson's first six months in charge was a blistering FA Cup run in which Willie Johnston shone like a beacon as Albion defeated Blackpool, Manchester United and Derby County on the way to a sixth-round meeting with the team who released a record proclaiming themselves "The best team in land", Cloughie's Nottingham Forest, at that time a side who were seemingly invincible. Johnston recalls, "We always felt we could win, even though they were top of the league. They were a good unit, but we thought that in certain areas, we had better individuals, and that if we could get at them one-to-one, we could do them. That was Ron's philosophy; go out and play. He had a tough time initially because we'd never really heard of him when he came, but he just let us keep doing what had worked for us. Big Ron was ideal for me at that time because I just wanted to entertain people which was what he wanted. I'd do a trick where I'd trap the ball with my backside, and when I did that, Cloughie was up off the bench going berserk, and once we'd wound him up, we felt we were on the way. Mick Martin put us one up early on, and I remember Big Cyrille going through for the second; I was thinking, "For God's sake, don't bloody miss that you big sod!" We could have won any cup game that year bar the semi final."

The semi final against Ipswich at Highbury was a disaster from start to finish, John Wile splitting his head open in the first few minutes trying, unsuccessfully, to prevent a Talbot goal. Wile played much of the game with his head swathed in bandages, blood seeping from a head wound, but few of his colleagues could find similar-blood-and thunder performances, on an oddly listless day when

15

Johnston also had to play with a dislocated shoulder picked up early on. Mick Martin was sent off as a late rally threatened to snatch an undeserved draw, but as it was, Bomber's late penalty was in vain and Albion went out 3-1. But the side regrouped to win four of the next five league games and end up sixth in the table. When Kenny Dalglish scored the only goal of the 1978 European Cup Final at Wembley to retain the trophy for Liverpool, it wasn't only the Scousers who were celebrating, for the Scotsman's goal meant Albion qualified for the UEFA Cup and a European adventure.

But before that, there was history to make in a much-further-flung corner of the globe.

CHAPTER TWO

VISIONS OF CHINA

Football is now the global game. With the 2002 World Cup held in Japan and Korea, with Manchester United and others regularly playing in the USA, in Hong Kong and elsewhere, football has colonised the world. The big names, the big teams and the big multinationals associated with football can now be found pretty well anywhere you go in the world. But it wasn't always so, for back in 1978, the beautiful game was very much the preserve of Europe and South America in particular, with the African nations slowly taking an increasing interest, leaving the Far East as a corner of the world virtually untouched by football.

It's not often that you get the opportunity to go into uncharted territory, but that was the privilege afforded the Albion when they were selected to go on tour to China, becoming the first English side ever to play in the Orient, though some suggest it was a last minute thing after the England team had pulled out of a similar trip. Post-season tours were a regular feature of football life before internationals made the fixture list so congested, but generally they were pretty relaxed affairs, a reward for players after the long, hard slog through the English winter, a chance to unwind and relax in the sunny climes of Spain or Florida perhaps. But China was something very different, and it certainly was never going to be a "let your hair down" kind of tour, as John Wile explains.

"It was very formal. Most trips were relaxed, but there were a lot of duties to be carried out on this one because we were representing English football and the FA, and Bert Millichip probably saw it as a feather in his cap in terms of his ambitions there. We had a lot of meetings with the Foreign Office before we went, telling us how to behave, and I remember one of the lads standing up and saying, "It'll be alright if we take our shirts off like we do when we go to Spain won't it?" That got a definite no! There was a lot of protocol to remember, and it was very tiring in a lot of ways, because we were away for three weeks. You perhaps appreciate it more and more as time goes on, looking back at how it's changed and that we did go at such a sensitive time, just after the Gang of Four had capitulated and with the students still protesting and revolting in some areas."

The students weren't the only ones as some of the players began to feel the pressure of being cooped up in hotel room. As Tony Brown says, "It was a hard tour at the end of a long season and to be honest most of us didn't really enjoy it very much. There was a lot of travelling involved, and we were looked upon as ambassadors for the country. But I never liked touring at the best of times so it wasn't really made for me!

"It was a very long trip, three weeks, a long, long flight to get there, and China wasn't really the best place to go 25 years ago anyway. There was nothing to do on the tour; it was very boring away from the playing side and it dragged on. At one stage we were taking the mickey out of ourselves with it all – I remember Mick Martin was sending suicide notes home to his wife because he was that fed up with it!"

Yet for all that it was tough tour, it was critical in the formation of the team that would carry the game to the rest of Division One in the following season, the footballing version of friendships forged in the heat of battle, though the discomfort suffered by the Albion players was rather easier to bear than that by real soldiers. Nevertheless, it was a month where those players really did come together as a unit, as John Wile explains.

"People think touring is brilliant, but because you're there to play, it's not a big jolly, it's not all shopping – not that there were any shops in China! They'd take us to Friendship Stores: small supermarkets with gifts laid out. But a lot of time was spent sitting in your room or the foyer of the hotel, and they were pretty basic at times. So we'd read or play cards, and that can get a bit tedious for a bunch of hyperactive people who want to get out and about.

"Those tours do bring people together because we were thrown into close proximity; we had to behave, and that brings a tremendous spirit. It was the kind of group where any bunch of the lads could have gone out and enjoyed a drink together, and that's not always the case because you don't always want to spend time with people you work with, but I think we genuinely did enjoy each other's company, which helped us get through it without going mad."

As did the football, for this was a side that genuinely loved to get on the pitch and play the game, wherever and whenever it could. The fact that there were five games ahead of them over a period of eleven days – ironically, ideal preparation for the fixture chaos that would ensue the following March and April – gave the players something to focus on. Their hosts, eager to please, also gave the Baggies the opportunity to take a look at what their domestic football was like before Albion took to the field themselves, the party going to a game on the eve of their own first appearance in China, as Wile remembers.

18

"We saw videos of games in China before we went out, where if a player was fouled, the game would stop and the player who'd committed the foul would make sure the other one was okay! When we got there, we went out to watch a local game in the stadium in Peking, 25,000 people in a 125,000 stadium. A guy got through on goal and missed and there were a few rumblings in the crowd, and then a message came over the tannoy to tell the crowd not to make so much noise because they were putting the players off!

"We were well-briefed over what to expect from the tour. We were told we had to do things right and we were told that the theme for the tour was "Friendship First, Competition Second." So we expected that when we played, and that game we watched didn't lead us to believe anything else. We played a Peking XI, I won the toss, we chose ends, they kicked off. They launched it down Derek Statham's throat like any side does from the kick off, hoof it out wide and press. Derek let it bounce to take it on the chest and their guy came at him, studs up, and took him in the throat! So we knew Friendship First, Competition Second was going to be misleading!"

Even Tony Brown, a self-confessed reluctant football tourist, found that there were moments to cherish from this tour, including a visit to one of the world's wonders. "Going to see the Great Wall of China was the highlight of the trip for me, it was a quite incredible sight. The funniest thing that I remember about it was Cliff Edwards who was with us he was a director at the time and he was wearing a pair of brand new shoes, so the soles were very slippy. We were walking uphill and he couldn't get any grip, and as we were walking, he'd take three steps forward and then slip half a dozen back! John Trewick wasn't very impressed with it, mind. He said on the TV programme, "Once you've seen one wall, you've seen 'em all!" That was typical of John, very dry sense of humour, he was just having a joke, and they took it out of context and put it in the film. If you mention it, John goes quiet even now!"

The film Bomber is referring to was made by the BBC for *The World About Us* series, another indication of just what a huge impact this tour was making, far beyond the sporting world. "That kept us going as well, the fact that they were filming it for the BBC, so we had a film crew and Julian Pettifer, the journalist, with us. It was interesting to be a part of that, and it broke up the monotony of it all. But like you saw on the TV, all we seemed to be doing was going to official functions all the while, visiting embassies and then going and visiting the communes that the people lived in. And the food wasn't the best, it was nothing like the Chinese food that you get used to in a restaurant in this country! We had to generate our own entertainment really, but I suppose that drew us even closer together.

"And looking back on it, we had some very interesting experiences. The crowds were massive, we got 90,000 when we played the national side, there was 80,000 at another game. The thing that I'll never forget, that stands out even now, was that the crowd were never allowed to make any noise at all, they weren't allowed to get excited. It was incredible. If they had the ball and got near our goal, the crowd would start making a noise, and as soon as they did, a voice would come over the loudspeaker system telling them to shut up and calm down! As soon as they heard that, it went back to deadly silence, it was eerie. At first we couldn't understand what was going on, but we were told afterwards that they weren't allowed to get excited. It was an eye-opener to see how the people were treated there in those days."

But that wasn't the only thing the TV cameras captured. Viewers in the UK had rarely had such an intimate glimpse of real life behind the "Bamboo Curtain" before, and that was fascinating. But just as groundbreaking was the fact that a real top English team were building their side around three black footballers, players who were glamorous, exciting and unutterably compelling. For a film director, this was visual manna from heaven, glorious and thought-provoking imagery – an English football team as strangers in this most foreign of lands, juxtaposed against images of three black men making their own journey into the heart of a foreign game where the white man's supremacy had been unchallenged since the sport began.

In the days when Starsky & Hutch dominated the TV screens, Laurie Cunningham may well have been the only man on the planet who was trendier, slicker and cooler than Huggy Bear. Watching Cyrille Regis' monumental physique trying to burst out of his shirt was like watching the great heavyweight boxer Joe Frazier getting really tetchy. And then there was Brendon Batson, sporting the kind of Afro that would have earned him a place in Earth, Wind & Fire, playing elegantly, talking articulately and quietly consigning every stupid racist stereotype to the dustbin where it belonged. These three were the greatest triumvirate to hit English football since the Holy Trinity of Best, Law and Charlton at Manchester United, and the BBC cameras caught them on the cusp of legend, as Tony Brown says.

"The whole "Three Degrees" thing really started on that trip I think, because that was when Brendon really started breaking into the team after Paddy Mulligan had left. The three of them got close and they loved being the focus of it. At the meals, there was a European table and a Chinese table, and there were only three of the boys who had the Chinese food every time and it was them three! I think the fact that the BBC were there built it up, because not only were we in a strange country but we had these three brilliant black players together at a time when there were hardly any black players in the game. That documentary just caught them right at the start of it all, breaking new ground. And what players they were to do it, absolutely superb all of them."

Albion found the competition less than taxing through the tour. Having beaten the Peking XI by three goals to one, the national side were next up in the same Workers Stadium in Peking, Ally Brown and Cyrille Regis providing a sign of the shape of things to come by providing the goals in a 2-0 win. Shanghai were next, losing by the same score as the Baggies did just enough to win the game without exerting themselves, Regis and Cunningham doing the damage this time. That was supposed to have been the end of the Chinese leg of the tour, but as John Wile notes, "The tour must have been a real success because, on the way back, they arranged another game in Canton in a hurry. Without exaggeration, when we got there the day before, the pitch had two-feet high of grass on it, it looked like a cornfield. They said they were getting it cut, and they took about six inches off and we tried to train on it, which was ridiculous. Finally they cut it again to a reasonable level, but they left big tractor furrows in the pitch! We beat them six nil. I actually scored so it must have been pretty easy!" The other scorers were the inevitable Regis – twice Cunningham, Bomber and, Mick Martin.

Kwantung Province having been suitably thumped, Albion bade farewell to China and a monumental and genuinely historic tour. Given the antics that footballers currently get up to - and get into trouble for - even in the most liberal of western cultures, the fact that it passed off without any major news stories making the front pages rather than the back ones is a credit to the players who went out there, and to the press who were a little more "on side" than might be the case today, as Wile admits.

"The press went with us, some big name journalists like Ian Wooldridge as well. If they'd worked to the standards of today, they'd have had some stories – not bad things, just bits of stupidity that you do when you get cabin fever, I suppose. Alistair Robertson loved to put water in people's beds so that they'd get soaked when they got in – childish, but when you're away, it breaks things up a bit! If he couldn't do that, he'd throw buckets of water. In Shanghai, he was waiting for Bryan Robson coming up in the lift. He'd got this spittoon – because spitting was acceptable – and it was full of spit, water, fag ends, all sorts of crap, and as the doors opened, he threw it. But it wasn't Bryan, it was Bert Millichip! So Bert just stood there, turned to me and said, "John, I think you'd better get the players to bed now." You'd not get away with that now, innocent fun, a bit silly but the kind of things that happen on tour. The other one was when we had a celebration in Shanghai the night before the game. We all felt rough the next day but we played and Wooldridge wrote, "Under the most difficult conditions yet, Albion won 2-0"! You'd get slaughtered now!"

Ally Robertson must have felt jinxed on that tour, for he was caught up in the middle of the one diplomatic faux pas of the trip as Tony Brown recalls. "We were playing cricket against the press on the hotel lawn in Shanghai the one day, and the press lads were doing alright. Ally was out on the boundary, and he might have helped himself to a can or two of lager while he was down there! Anyway, we were getting beat, so for a joke, he got a white towel and ran it up the flagpole to say we were surrendering. But apparently, in China, that's the signal for national mourning and all the hotel staff came racing outside, shouting and screaming; it was mayhem! In the end, the representative from the British Embassy who'd been travelling with us had to step in and calm things down, but Ally nearly got his marching orders over that one!"

One player who kept his head down on this tour was Ally Brown, for he was loath to repeat the mistakes he'd made under Ronnie Allen a year earlier. "We went to Alicante pre-season in 1977 and me and Ronnie had a bust-up when I was a bit naughty, a bit unprofessional. If Ronnie had stayed, my days were certainly numbered. We didn't get on, to the extent I ended up playing right-back in the reserves, and I even spoke to Bury who were in the Third Division, but I thought that although I seemed finished here, I was still better than that. And then Ronnie went off to Saudi Arabia at the Christmas and it was another rebirth of my career after that. But that's the game. Some managers like you and some don't, and if they don't like you, you don't like them!

"But once Big Ron came in, I was back in the picture, though Willie Johnston always reckons that it was him who got me back in under Ron. Me and Bud were good mates. I was his chauffeur, I picked him up every day, so maybe that was why he wanted me back in, to make sure he kept his driver! Ron wanted somebody to play with Cyrille, and Willie apparently said to him that he ought to give me a crack at it. Willie was a one-off, different class, you never knew what you'd get from him. He started a fight with me one day in training. Just a five-a-side and I must have kicked him, so he just turned round and started punching me and the lads had to pull him off. And I'm driving him home! Two minutes later, it was all, "Sorry big man, don't know what I was doing there!" That was Willie!"

Yet just as Ally Brown was revitalising his Albion career in China, Willie's was ending half a world away in Argentina. Since Atkinson had arrived at The Hawthorns, Johnston had been perhaps Albion's best player, revelling in the confidence Atkinson had in him and in attacking football based on getting the ball wide whenever possible. He had been the central figure in the FA Cup run, his electrifying form cementing his place in the Scottish squad that was heading for South America and the 1978 World Cup under Ally McLeod. Under the garrulous self-publicist of a manager – a poor man's Atkinson – Scotland expected its players to return with the World Cup, for they were on the match with Ally's Army, their hubris extending to a bon voyage party at Hampden. Johnston was a central figure in that team, the manufacturer of the bullets for Joe Jordan and Kenny Dalglish, and while Scottish optimism was wildly overplayed, in a group that included Peru, Holland and Iran, qualification for the second phase looked odds on.

21

The campaign opened with a nightmarish 3-1 defeat at the hands of an ageing Peruvian side, Don Masson missing a crucial penalty for a team in which every player, Willie included, had a stinker, and his mood was hardly improved when he was required to stay behind to provide a sample for the drugs testers. Nothing other than an inconvenience, within 24 hours that sample had turned Willie's life inside out as he tested positive for fencamfamin, which FIFA described later as a "harmful and pernicious" drug, in spite of the fact that great swathes of the British population were taking it at the same time as Willie, in the same way – through the over-the-counter hay fever remedy, Reactivan.

Willie was told that he'd never play for Scotland again, a far harsher punishment than FIFA's eventual sentence, which ruled him out of international competition – including the UEFA Cup – for twelve months. He returned home to England to find that most of his Albion colleagues were off on holiday, having gone away straight after getting back from China. Fortunately for Johnston, at least Ron Atkinson was still in the country, as John Wile says. "Big Ron met him at the airport on the way back and made a joke of it all, didn't take it too seriously, and that defused it a bit, went on about Willie getting a sponsorship deal with Boots! Today, Willie would have been crucified.

"From what he told me about what went on in Argentina, he was very disappointed with the Scottish FA who just hung him out to dry. It was hard after that, the crowds got on his back, and he was never the same, which was sad. He was my favourite player. I've seen Laurie do things that to this day I've never seen another player do, he was incredible, but when Willie got the ball, the hairs would stand up on the back of my neck because I never knew what he was going to do. So quick, two good feet, go outside or inside, wonderful to watch. Wingers aren't often consistent, but over a period of time, Willie was much more consistent than Laurie, who would go from incredible heights to being anonymous, where Willie always contributed something."

Tony Brown was also a fully paid up member of the Willie Johnston fan club. "He was a great friend of mine, brilliant lad and he was devastated because he was labelled a cheat and really he'd done nothing. They called it drugs but all he'd taken was a hay fever remedy. The club doctor told me afterwards that there were about 400 things on the banned list for that World Cup and some were just stupid things like cough mixtures and things for headaches, tablets you take as part of everyday life here. But they were on the list and Willie ended up getting slaughtered for it."

Wile continues the sad story, adding, "Willie lost his confidence after Argentina and that was the end because he was a confidence player. He'd get suspended for daft things, but I always used to say to whichever manager, "Monday or Tuesday, tell Willie he's playing on Saturday." Otherwise he'd be a bag of nerves all week. Not that there was a question that he'd be playing, but he didn't think that way. He needed to be told he was good and that he was important to us.

"Saying that, things were changing and I'm sure that Willie missed out by not going to China because a team had formed there with Laurie at the centre of a lot of things, and that alone would have made it hard for him to get back in. And we were becoming a bit more ruthless in our play. Willie was a fabulous character, but for him, football was just something to be enjoyed, and I think there was a growing realisation that we were on the brink of something here. Ron still wanted us to entertain, but he also wanted us to win."

"After we beat Forest in the FA Cup," recalls Tony Brown, "Brian Clough said to Ron that he was a brave manager to be playing with two out-and-out wingers so often, and I think going into the new season, maybe Ron felt he could only have the one, the way Cloughie had John Robertson. In China, Laurie had come in and cemented his place in the side. I felt sorry for Willie because he was innocent and it ended his career. He was magic to have in the side, the opposition were frightened to death of him, and that made it easier because they'd double up on him and give us space. But if you'd got to replace Willie, you couldn't have had anybody better than Laurie."

Johnston's UEFA Cup ban certainly did him no favours either, but in June 1978, Ron Atkinson was solely concerned with keeping the magical winger out of the public eye. Decisions on who would play where could keep for a few weeks yet.

22

CHAPTER THREE

OF THESE, HOPE

There's little doubt that, at The Hawthorns, the 1978/79 season dawned with greater expectation surrounding it than any season since the halcyon days of the late 1960s when they routinely climaxed with a cup final appearance.

In the two years since the Baggies had climbed back into the big time, they had put together as impressive a first-team squad as anything beyond the seemingly impenetrable citadel of Anfield, so much so that we didn't trouble the transfer market over the summer, Ron Atkinson's only signing being the introduction of Colin Addison as his assistant. Addison, a crucial factor in Hereford United's FA Cup exploits of the early 1970s and their ascent to league football, was plying his trade at Newport County and had actually been one of the names on Albion's managerial shortlist when Ronnie Allen left for the Middle East. Addison was perhaps a less excitable figure than Big Ron and offered a steadying influence on the manager, reining in some of his more attacking impulses.

That said, the trip to China in particular had seen Atkinson begin to put his stamp on his side, the fact that he and his squad were in such close proximity allowing him to get across his philosophy on the game. It also gave him time to watch his back four in action away from the heat of First Division battle and to realise just what a bedrock they would be for him. Batson, Statham, Wile and Robertson were a match for anything in the land as a fearsome and fearless combination. With that in his mind, Atkinson was able to allow his instincts to take over and make subtle, but crucial, adjustments to the team.

The side that went on the 1978 cup run had certainly been based on forward play, but there remained traces of the slow, methodical build up from the Giles era. Atkinson did not want possession for its own sake, but wanted something more dynamic, quicker, slicker. He wanted the side to live off the pace of Regis and Ally Brown, to hit those front two earlier so they could destroy stretched defences, rather than trying to fight their way through massed ranks, who had time to fall back into position under the Giles approach of pass-pass-pass. Giles' approach had been vital in getting Albion moving in the right direction again, but Atkinson was looking for the next step in the side's evolution, which saw the end of players of lesser pace such as Mick Martin and Paddy Mulligan.

"Ron added Brendon to replace Paddy Mulligan, to push it on again," according to John Wile. "Paddy couldn't run! Yet every time you looked up he was past the halfway line waiting for the ball off Gilesy! Great brain, passed it well, good attitude, but the biggest mickey taker. He and Ron didn't get on though; Paddy took to calling him the Incredible Bulk and the Towering Inferior, so that was that! The two didn't get on, so Brendon was in, and that added more pace to the side, which was crucial. Great pace up front, not blistering in the middle because you don't need it so much there, but quick enough, and we weren't slow across the back either, we were rarely caught short by anybody.

"Ron didn't make major changes, he just encouraged us to play a bit more quickly and a bit more directly. Under John, we wouldn't go forward if we couldn't pass it safely, we'd go backwards or sideways, just to make sure we didn't give the ball away. Ron encouraged us to hit the front players a bit quicker. We had pace to burn up front in Laurie and Cyrille, and Ron wanted us to use that, to hit them early and then support them, and that added a fresh dimension. We were becoming more attack-minded naturally, with the arrival of those two, with Derek Statham, Bryan Robson was maturing and Brendon came in."

As far as pace went, you couldn't have got off to a quicker start to a season than the Baggies did at home to Ipswich Town. The Baggies were out of the blocks inside the first minute, Ally Brown grabbing the first goal of the season anywhere in the country to give Albion a lead. That in itself was a huge relief, for the side didn't go into the new season in the greatest heart after a mixed pre-season programme had seen Albion surrender the Tennant-Caledonian Cup they had won twelve months earlier in the four-team tournament at Ibrox, losing to Southampton on penalties and then to Hearts in a third-place play-off game, these fixtures perhaps most notable for the fact that trialist goalkeeper Bruce Grobbelaar was on the Albion bench. A couple of poor performances in Syria followed, so it was important that Albion hit their straps right from the outset, Ally Brown's goal settling a few early nerves.

Ipswich hit back with a Clive Woods equaliser, but this was to be Albion's day, and it was the other Brown, Tony, who began what would be an Indian Summer of a season for him, scoring the winner from close range in front of the Smethwick End. It's a day Bomber still recalls with affection. "We couldn't have had a better start to things. Straight out of the box, we were a goal up against Ipswich, which was nice after they'd knocked us out of the FA Cup in the semi final the year before. Ally Brown set us off, and I got the winner later on, and we finished up beating them 2-1, which was important for us. If the first game goes the right way, it sets the tone, gets everybody up-and-running for the season. Ally did great for us that year. He didn't get the credit he deserved, but he was a brilliant player up front, unselfish, did a lot of running and he was a great foil for Cyrille, helped him mature a lot as a player.

"The season took off from there, all one way after that, and it was marvellous to be involved. Every player had class, the confidence was high, the dressing room was great. The chemistry was perfect, everybody fitted in, defence was solid, midfield was sound, just a great team all the way through, a delight to play in it."

Right off the bat, things had changed in the composition and chemistry of that team. Batson had slotted into Paddy Mulligan's right-back position, Ally Brown was undisputed first choice alongside Cyrille Regis up front, and, perhaps most telling of all, the ideal of playing with two wingers had been largely shelved, Laurie Cunningham getting the nod ahead of Willie Johnston. In an era when a blind eye was turned to East German women athletes who were more masculine than Geoff Capes as a result of their steroid abuse, Willie's Albion career was all but over because of a couple of hay fever tablets.

That said, it remains a moot point as to whether or not Johnston would have been able to retain his place in a side that only had room for one maverick. Atkinson was determined that his midfield should include Len Cantello, an iron man who could still pass superbly, as well as the emerging brilliance of Bryan Robson, a player you simply couldn't leave out of the team, while John Trewick was solid back up for either of those two. With Bomber Brown rolling back the years and irreplaceable as a goalscoring midfielder, he wasn't going to be shouldered aside by anybody, which left a straight fight between Cunningham and Johnston. A pre-season ankle injury did the Scot few favours, and as the season started in earnest, he was allotted the number twelve shirt, game after game.

Cunningham had one huge advantage up his sleeve – his availability for the UEFA Cup. That might just have been the clincher, enabling Atkinson to play a settled side, game after game. He did just that in the first three games of the season as maximum points were harvested, Albion winning in London, a rarity in itself, as they beat QPR by a single goal, then thumping four goals past Bolton without reply, the first three coming in 25 minutes.

Over the course of just those first 270 minutes of football, it was apparent that here was an Albion side that was not merely as good as the team that had reached the FA Cup semi finals the year before. It was better. It had added a new attacking thrust to the way it played its football, producing a style of play that was almost unheard of in the negative, dour, defence-minded era ushered in by Arsenal's double winners at the start of the decade. Where most football teams in England played in a drab monochrome, Albion played in vibrant colour, the thick navy blue-and-white stripes toying with dreary defences, the Samba beat of Albion's fabled "Three Degrees" serving up a footballing cocktail that took the country aback. It genuinely was just like watching Brazil for a while.

By the time Bolton were beaten, Alistair Brown had scored three goals, Tony Brown, Laurie Cunningham and Cyrille Regis all weighing in with another each, as goals were shared around the team – and the opposition, as QPR presented us with our winner there, courtesy of an own goal. The demolition of Bolton in particular was a breathtaking affair as they were simply crushed by quick movement, sharp passing, clever wing play and great finishing, Regis finishing off the slaughter with his first goal of the season. But to Cyrille, it was just another day at the office – he expected Albion to hit those high standards week in, week out.

"We just set off like a train at the start of that season. It was just a point where we stepped up a gear because that side had pretty much been together a year, we were comfortable with one another. A lot of the boys had been together since the Johnny Giles era and a good foundation had been set in and that was a rarity even then, teams didn't stay together for long, managers didn't get time with them. Ok, we had a turnover of managers with Giles leaving, then Ronnie Allen only staying a short while, but the team stayed in place, and then Big Ron came in and put his stamp on it.

"The key was that the team stayed together, about 14 players that didn't really change much over three seasons. Going to China had helped pull us closer together, and we had a great team spirit. You get consistency from that togetherness and we were just ready to explode as a team, we gelled together that season, and looking back on it, it was fantastic from the off. We went out on the pitch and felt we couldn't get beaten."

Nor could they in those initial weeks. The vagaries of cup draws and replays would mean that, by season's end, Albion would play Leeds United on seven occasions, the first coming in a dour League Cup tie at The Hawthorns which ended in goalless stalemate, the same scoreline achieved at Nottingham Forest's City ground the following Saturday. Brian Clough's side had been the surprise League Champions the season before, but they'd got off to a slow start to the new campaign, drawing all their first three First Division games, a record that would be extended to six draws out of the first seven, less of a penalty in the days when you only got two points for a win. That they got their fourth draw in a row was thanks largely to the quality of Peter Shilton as the Baggies hammered the home side, Shilton underlining why, at that time, he was perhaps the best goalkeeper in the world and the single most important player in Forest's Championship win.

It was three goalless draws in a row for the Albion after the League Cup replay at Elland Road, while the unbeaten start stretched to seven games, though this time the Baggies were disappointed to drop a home point to Norwich. That was perhaps the last hurrah for the 4-2-4 system that Atkinson still toyed with, Johnston playing his third successive game in the same eleven as Cunningham, thanks largely to injury to Tony Brown. An unexpected result it may have been, but Albion were lucky to get the draw, Bryan Robson's last-gasp equaliser rescuing something from a game where they had earlier been cruising. Defensive slips had been costly, particular as the side was exposed for the second Canaries goal, and this didn't go unnoticed by Atkinson. A cavalier side Albion might have been, but they weren't going to be suicidal. A rethink was in order as they embarked on their first competitive European game since losing to Dunfermline in the third round of the European Cup Winners' Cup in February 1969, since when, English clubs had begun to dominate, an optimistic omen for the club as it set off for a game in Turkey.

Back in 1978, we hadn't heard much about this club called Galatasaray or the welcome they put on...

26

CHAPTER FOUR

MOVING FORCE

The roll call of English successes in Europe since Manchester United first claimed the Champions' Cup for the nation at Wembley in May 1968 was very much at odds with the national side's decidedly underwhelming performance thereafter. The legendary Bill Shankly had taken Liverpool to UEFA Cup triumph in 1973, laying the groundwork for Bob Paisley to lead his side to the same title in 1976 and then the European Cup itself in successive years, 1977 and 1978. Leeds United (twice), Arsenal, Newcastle and Tottenham had all won the UEFA Cup or its Inter-Cities Fairs Cup forerunner – Spurs beating Wolves in a two-legged final, an achievement for which Albion fans were truly grateful – while the Cup Winners' Cup had been won by Manchester City and by Chelsea, who had even managed to overcome the mighty Real Madrid in the final.

English domination of the top trophy was to continue some years longer courtesy of Nottingham Forest, Liverpool again and then Aston Villa, and the European Cup remained the pinnacle of achievement in club football, the holy grail for any team that truly wanted to lay claim to being the best. And yet, as Shankly himself had said, it was the UEFA Cup that provided the truest test of a side's credentials, for if nothing else, there was an extra round of competition to navigate. In addition, these were the days when you actually had to have won your national championship in order to qualify for the European Champions' Cup – sounds like a good plan doesn't it? Rather than there being a surfeit of sides sloshing around that competition, those who had finished in the upper echelons of Europe's leagues found themselves fighting it out in the UEFA Cup instead.

So, instead of simply doing battle with AC Milan in the European Cup, those qualifying for the UEFA Cup might be pitted against Juventus, Inter Milan and Roma or Real Madrid, Atletico Madrid and Valencia instead of just Barcelona, Cologne and Borussia Moenchengladbach rather than simply Bayern Munich. Very often too, those that contested the European Cup were sides that had reached their peak in winning their domestic league, had perhaps lost the edge of their hunger, were possibly on the slide. On the other hand, those in the UEFA Cup were often the coming sides, those ready to take charge of their domestic leagues, those maturing into formidable footballing outfits. Teams, in short, like Albion.

English clubs were no longer cowed by the prospect of continental opposition, but as Albion started their UEFA Cup campaign with a trip to Turkey, few gave the club much hope of lifting the trophy the following May. Which gave Ron Atkinson all the excuse he needed to treat the trip as a bit of a break from the more important demands of the domestic game. That relaxed attitude was a huge fillip to the squad, for otherwise they would have flown out to Turkey under the weight of expectation, for, typical of the insular attitude of the English, few pundits believed that any club from Turkey could possibly defeat a footballing team of any quality – that's to say an English team. These were Third World nonentities, there as cannon fodder: a stupid, blinkered view that helps explain why it is that English football has spent the last twenty years watching helplessly as other nations have overtaken us. Turkey was emerging as a footballing nation, and, especially on their own patch, their clubs deserved to be taken very seriously indeed.

Colin Addison did Albion's homework on Galatasaray, for the club was in no mood to allow this European campaign to become a one-game wonder, the players relishing what for many was a first real taste of international competition, as Cyrille Regis remembers. "The European campaign was something special for all of us, a bonus really on top of the league. It was a great opportunity to go abroad, to play against different kinds of opposition and stretch yourselves as footballers, learn more about the game. It was something we loved doing."

For the likes of John Wile and Alistair Robertson, this was a rare treat at the other end of their careers. Neither were to win international honours – incomprehensibly so in the case of Robertson given the quality of competition among other Scottish defenders – so the UEFA Cup was a rare opportunity to test their mettle, and their very British virtues, against the best the continent had to offer. And it was a testing trip in every respect, as Wile recalls. "We should have played them in Istanbul but we didn't, it was in Izmir down the coast, because they'd had supporter problems and UEFA had said they couldn't play at their home ground. We got there on the Monday for a Wednesday game and everything was fine. The coach would park in front of the hotel, we'd get on it, drive up the main road, turn right, go to the stadium, a five-minute journey to training. The day of the game, we got in the coach and for some reason – you can draw your own conclusions! - the driver went a different way and we found ourselves in the middle of all the match traffic. People were just parking their cars in the middle of the road, getting out in front of us, so the bus would stop, reverse, edge round them. It took us 90 minutes to get there!"

As Cyrille Regis says, with masterful understatement, "It was a really interesting experience to go to play Galatasaray in the first round. Culturally it was very different. Then when we got stuck on the bus on the way to the game, it got nasty, their supporters were banging on the side of the bus and all sorts. Eventually, Mr. Lucas, who was one of the directors, had to get off the coach and walk in front of it to help clear a way through the crowds!"

28

Albion hammered the Turkish side 3-1 on their patch, against the team whose ground is now littered with "Welcome to hell" placards if ever an English team dares venture there, Regis saying, "It probably wasn't as hostile as you see it today, but there was definitely a real atmosphere about the place, which made it a very special win for us." Two goals from Laurie Cunningham and another from Bryan Robson finished them off, making Albion the first English team to beat Galatasaray in Turkey, and they remained the only English winners there until Chelsea repeated the feat in October 1999 with a yet more emphatic 5-0 win. And if Chelsea had Gianfranco Zola that night, the Baggies had their own magician 25 years back. Laurie Cunningham.

Regis recalls, "Nobody ever entertained the public more than Laurie Cunningham. He was like Thierry Henry; he was graceful, good on the eye. He wasn't ragged, wasn't raw; he was smooth, very balletic, great balance, such poise. Nothing encapsulated that better than the 5-3 game at Manchester United and the commentary that went with it. "There goes Laurie Cunningham again, pace and grace and style." That was Laurie; that was what he was: such a special player."

So how was it that Laurie didn't break into the England side ahead of Peter Barnes of Manchester City?

"The lads at Albion never did get the England call-ups that maybe they deserved. Bryan Robson had to wait a long time and didn't become a regular until he went to Manchester United, Derek Statham hardly got any recognition, and Laurie, even though he became the first black player to play for England at under-21 level, had to wait a long time for his chance at senior level. It's hard to understand why really. But England had a settled side, the likes of Keegan, Coppell, Mariner, Brooking, Watson, they didn't make the changes they do now so it was hard to break into the side and show them what you could do. It took me five years to get a full cap and that was just the way it was, you had to be consistent over a period of years before getting in."

Cunningham was the key to that victory, but impressive as it was, it barely registered on the media's Richter Scale at the time as John Wile remembers. "At the time, people in this country used to dismiss teams from places like Turkey, but as we've seen since, going to Galatasaray is a difficult business. People didn't appreciate what a great win that was for us out there. So after that, to win 3-1 was a terrific result. Big Ron was spot on in his attitude, saying we were there to enjoy ourselves, to play good football, not get too worried about the UEFA Cup, and so we were relaxed, we did what we were good at and won. We kept it tight, but then when you've got Laurie, Cyrille, Ally and Tony in your team, the opposition couldn't attack us too much because we'd hit them on the break. We were delighted with the win, it was a big night for us, so much so that maybe one or two players celebrated a little bit too much on the way home!"

That much was underlined less than 72 hours later when the Baggies suffered their first defeat of the season on Derby's notorious Baseball Ground pitch, though the surface could not be blamed on this occasion, a September skirmish worlds away from dealing with the quagmire it was traditionally reduced to by the new year. But the players looked leg-weary after the arduous trip to Turkey and Albion were almost out of the game before it had begun, two down inside the first quarter, and though they fought back, a 3-2 defeat left them in a familiar position in the league table – looking up at Liverpool. Bob Paisley's awesome red machine had made a storming start to the league season, reeling off six wins out of six, though their grip on the European Cup had been dislodged a little by a first-round, first-leg slip-up at Nottingham Forest of all places, Clough's side winning 2-0, inspired by a young man who six months earlier had been playing non-league football in Long Eaton, Garry Birtles.

With that in mind, Liverpool were an even more formidably terrifying outfit than usual. They wanted their title back from Forest and had spanked all comers in those first half-dozen fixtures, knocking in 20 goals, conceding just two in the process. The visit of Liverpool, even so early in the season, before you expected them to really hit their stride, was always one viewed with a mixture of anticipation and trepidation. With Albion visibly maturing before the supporters' eyes, Liverpool offered the crucial yardstick. Just how good were Albion these days?

Early on, the answer was simple. Not as good as Liverpool, as Ron Atkinson recalls. "That was one of the best games of the season, no question about it. But for the first 20 minutes, if we hadn't been such a good side, we'd have been 6-0 down because the quality of their play in that period was incredible." John Wile remembers it very much the same way, adding, "That season, I think Liverpool were probably as good a team as any there has ever been in English football, they were probably at their absolute best at that time. They had Dalglish, Clemence, Souness, Kennedy, Thompson, McDermott, Neal, incredible players; everywhere you looked they were quality, and to have to take that on was a huge task.

"There was an air about them, and most teams were beaten before they went on the pitch, and that takes years to achieve. That's probably the hardest part about going from being a good team to being something special. All the top sides have that belief. The likes of Arsenal and United have it now. You're psychologically beaten before you kick a ball. But we'd developed so much that we had the confidence in ourselves so that we could go to Anfield or have them at The Hawthorns, know we could give them a good game and expect to get something from it. But that day, they battered us for about 20 minutes, we didn't get out of our half, they passed it, and I remember saying to Alistair Robertson, "Have they got more players than us?" It felt like they had two men extra, but we came in at half-time at 0-0 and Big Ron came in and said, "There's not another team in Europe that could have held onto Liverpool today. That's been fantastic. You're such a good team, you've survived the best they can throw at you." Ron made us feel that Liverpool had blown themselves out, that we could get something out of the game. We'd started to come into it late on in the first half and we slowly pushed them back and started to play the game in their half."

As Atkinson continues, "We stayed in the game, got in front, had a really good goal by Cyrille disallowed for offside and we were well on top, going away from Liverpool, which was something a bit special. Then we threw it away with that daft equalizer. Tony Godden did his famous trick of rolling the ball out only for Kenny Dalglish to appear from behind him, nick the ball and score. Terrific game of football though." Godden's legendary lapse came as Albion looked to have the game under control. The 'keeper had gathered the ball and was simply dribbling it to the edge of the area prior to picking it up to take his goal kick, but what he failed to notice was that Kenny Dalglish had run off the pitch in the previous Liverpool attack. As Godden rolled the ball, the Scottish international raced back onto the field, stole the ball off his toes and stuck it into the back of the net. The crestfallen Godden was lucky that his error happened in front of the Brummie – had it happened at the Smethwick End, packed as it was with gleeful Scousers, his humiliation would have been unbearable. But it was to Albion's credit that, in spite of such a howler against the best in Europe, they regrouped and went on to see out the game, gaining a creditable draw, a result that Wile says was, "A huge one for us. It gave us confidence going on in the season."

The following Wednesday, Galatasaray were despatched with nonchalance, another 3-1 win closing the game out 6-2 on aggregate as Liverpool tumbled out of the European Cup at Anfield, Forest pulling off the shock of the season; and reminding everyone that they were now dealing with that most dangerous of footballing animals, a wounded Liverpool. In those circumstances, all Albion could do was to keep winning, and they did just that, sending Chelsea crashing into the bottom two with an emphatic 3-1 win at Stamford Bridge, Albion coming from behind to cruise to victory courtesy of goals from Regis, Wile and a very special goal for Bomber – his 208th in the league for the Baggies, matching Ronnie Allen's record.

"It was a bit of a relief because I'd gone a few games without getting a goal – I missed a couple of them through injury, but I hadn't scored since I got the winner against Ipswich on the first day of the season. You try not to dwell on the fact that you're so close to the record, you try to just carry on playing, but of course, you do think about it, it's always there because people are forever bringing it up, be it the papers, supporters or whatever. So it is always in the back of your mind and it's a great relief when you can finally get there and put it to rest. I remember it ever so well, it will always stick in my mind because you can't get away from it, it's a proud moment, a big thing to achieve.

We took a quick free kick and I thumped it in and we did it that quick that the TV cameras missed it! It's on the *Atkinson Era* DVD but you don't see the goal because we were so fast! Bryan Robson put his hand on the ball then rolled it through, I made a quick run before they got sorted out and stuck it away past Peter Bonetti. And it was a great win for us as well, kept the momentum going."

That it did, for as September reached its close, the Baggies were ensconced in third place, four points behind Liverpool whose only dropped point had come at The Hawthorns. A decent opening salvo, but things were starting to get a little hectic.

And then it snowed. Cantello, Ally Brown, Robson, Regis, Cunningham, The Hawthorns, January 1st 1979
(Picture: Laurie Rampling)

Albion's number one: Tony Godden
(Picture: Laurie Rampling)

They shall not pass: Alistair Robertson
(Picture: Laurie Rampling)

The first degree: Laurie Cunningham
(Picture: Laurie Rampling)

The third degree: Brendon Batson
(Picture: Laurie Rampling)

The second degree: Cyrille Regis
(Picture: Laurie Rampling)

Just Popped it in: Another goal for Bryan Robson
(Picture: Laurie Rampling)

Albion's greatest ever? Bryan Robson
(Picture: WBA Archive)

There's only one Derek Statham
(Picture: Laurie Rampling)

Mr. Post Man: John Wile
(Picture: Laurie Rampling)

In the short shorts: Ron Atkinson holds forth, Colin
Addison, Mick Martin and trialist Bruce Grobbelaar stay
in the background, July 1978 (Picture: WBA Archive)

"Oh, sort it out for yourselves!" Atkinson leaves Robson, Batson, Wile, Mills and Regis to their own devices,
extra-time v Leeds, March 1st 1979 (Picture: Laurie Rampling)

"Leave the Albion, would you!" Regis realises Cantello is on his way, Len Cantello testimonial game, May 1979
(Picture: Laurie Rampling)

It takes an army of four men to stop Ally Brown, Albion v Arsenal, April 14th 1979
(Picture: Laurie Rampling)

"That's not John Wile!" Alistair Robertson gets a new defensive partner (Picture: Laurie Rampling)

Cyrille!!!!! Another one for Regis
(Picture: Laurie Rampling)

"You distract him and I'll score." Cyrille Regis and Ally Brown, a striking partnership
(Picture: Laurie Rampling)

中、英足球友谊比赛名单

(一九七八年五月十七日下午四时)

裁判员：太　　勒（英）

巡边员：派　　利（英）　崔　宝　印

JACK CHEI PAO YIN

英国布朗米奇队　　　　北　京　队
CHIE SEI LIN

	教练员：	阿	特	金	森		教练员：	曾	习	麟			CHEN WEN KENG
		赖		特				成	文	宽			
GODDEN	运动员：	1	戈		登		运动员：	1	王	俊	生	WANG SINSHEN
BATSON		2	巴	特	森			0	张		路	CITANG LU
STATHAM		3	斯	特	瑟 姆			2	郎	作	亮	LOUNG CHIEH / LIAN y
T. BROWN		4	布		朗			3	温		远	WEN YUAN
WILE		5	怀		尔			4	夏	宝	柱	SHIH PAO CHU
ROBERTSON		6	鲁	宾	逊			5	赵	立	华	CHAOLI HWA
MARTIN		7	马		丁			6	贾	广	拓	CHIH KWANG TO
Rwa ROBSON		8	罗	布	森			7	刘	德	利	LIU TEH LI
REGIS		9	里	吉	斯			8	洪	元	硕	HUNG YUNG SHU
A BROWN		10	阿·布		朗			9	李	维	霄	LI WEI SHAU
CUNNINGHAM		11	坎	宁	安			10	李	维	淼	LI WEI MAO
HUGES		12	休		斯			11	沈	祥	福	SHENG CHIAN FU
LOVERIDGE			洛 夫 里 奇					12	张	东	平	CHANG TUNG PING
MONAGHAN			萨 默 菲 尔 德					13	沈		扬	SHENG YUNG
LOVERIDGE			莫	纳	汉			14	殷	迠	华	IN CHIEN HWA
SUMMERFIELD			特 里 威 克					15	张	金	望	CHANG JIN HONG
			格		鲁			16	谷	大	泉	KOO TAI CHIEN
								17	田	继	业	CHENKI TEN
								18	孟	昭	金	MENG CHAO KING
								19	刘	利	福	LIU LI FU

An unusual Chinese menu. Official team sheet, Peking XI v Albion, May 17th 1978
(WBA Archive)

CHAPTER FIVE

CATCH THE FALL

Once upon a time, domestic cup ties were allowed to be played to their conclusion, replay after replay if necessary, with none of this messing about with silver goals, golden goals or penalty shootouts. It had its downside though, for because of the demands of the rest of the fixture list, just 48 hours after Albion had beaten Chelsea, they were on the field again, at Maine Road, to take on Leeds United on neutral ground, in front of a paltry crowd of 8,164 in a second replay of their League Cup second-round tie, the winners scheduled to play in the third round on the Wednesday! 210 minutes of football across two games between the two sides had failed to yield a single goal, but the deadlock was finally broken after 33 minutes of the Manchester game when Paul Hart, later to find fame as Nottingham Forest's boss, scrambled home the only goal. Albion's disappointment was deep and genuine, but with a UEFA Cup campaign and a league challenge to attend to, it was a result that did little long-term damage.

Its short-term impact was more serious though as, on the following Saturday, the below-par Baggies slithered to another 1-0 defeat, this time at The Hawthorns against Tottenham, inspired for the first time that season by a midfielder who would go on to become an Albion legend a decade later, Osvaldo Ardiles. The Argentine had been the brains behind his nation's World Cup triumph that summer, when he had been the arch provider for another superstar who would soon cross Albion's path, Mario Kempes. But there was little South American swagger in this game, Spurs shutting up shop after Peter Taylor scored a breakaway after just four minutes, 'keeper Barry Daines, the man charged with the unenviable task of replacing the great Pat Jennings in the Tottenham goal, enjoying an inspired afternoon as Albion toiled in vain to get back on terms. It was a devastating reverse which saw the side slip to sixth place in the division, losing yet further ground to Liverpool who won again – 4-1 at Norwich's Carrow Road. Above West Brom also stood the big guns Everton and Forest, both still unbeaten, Manchester United and the more unlikely figures of Coventry City.

33

If the putative title challenge was going to endure beyond these opening weeks of the season, it was vital that Albion got things back on the rails with a win in the next game, but the omens were anything but promising with the side contemplating their fourth game against Leeds United inside seven weeks. Albion hadn't managed a goal in five hours of cup tie football and this time were faced by a trip to Elland Road in what was a must-win game. After just 20 minutes, the former Aberdeen winger Arthur Graham, always a thorn in Albion's side, put the home side ahead, but crucially, Tony Brown got West Brom back on terms just before the interval, a vital break given that his side were very much on the backfoot in the game as Ron Atkinson admits.

"When we had that team, we'd go away and maybe for an hour or so, we'd soak it up. I remember going to Leeds and they gave us a real battering and Wile and Robertson especially just took it, everything they could throw at us, and kept us in the game. Then, in the closing stages, Cyrille knocked a couple in and won the match, took all the headlines. Those lads at the back were the ones that gave us the foundation and allowed the flair players to go and do their stuff and win games for us – if we'd been three down at Leeds like we could have been, the likes of Cyrille couldn't have done anything about it."

The more observant will have noticed that though Regis got the important winning goals in the last few minutes, it was Bomber who got the first, a goal which made him Albion's greatest ever goalscorer in league football, with 209 to his credit. It remains a very proud moment for Tony, one he relishes still today.

"To be honest, the record looked miles away when Don Howe was here, but once John Giles got me going again, I started closing in on it. Equalling it was the hard thing, but having got that one at Chelsea, the next away game, straight out of the box, I broke it in front of the TV cameras and that was a great feeling, to go past Ronnie Allen's record, especially as it was only in my very early days that I was an out-and-out striker. After that I was converted to an attacking midfielder, even going back to Jimmy Hagan's time, so I got the majority of goals from midfield. That suited me because I wasn't one for playing with my back to goal, I liked to have the play in front of me, see things from deep, so coming from midfield was my real strength – I suppose Paul Scholes does the same sort of job nowadays.

"To score as many goals as I did, pretty much all from a midfield position, was an added bonus I suppose, because you don't get the chances the centre forwards get. Obviously it's harder to score from midfield, you have to do a lot more defensive work, so I am proud of the number I managed to get. Especially later on in my career, it was a real out-and-out midfield job under Johnny Giles and Ron Atkinson. It wasn't one of these free roles behind the front two that a lot play now, it was a proper midfield job, winning the ball, using it and trying to help out in defence and attack. Right from when I started in the 1960s though, it was always instilled into me that you'd got a job to do as a defender when needs be. You had a player in the opposition who you were up against and you had to stop him just like he was trying to stop you. I never had the luxury that some have of just playing in the hole and floating around.

34

"There's not many of that type of player about now – in my time Martin Peters was the obvious comparison for making late runs into the box and getting on the end of things. Gilesy stopped me advancing so much for a time; he educated me in picking my runs rather than going every time so as to preserve your energy, which was important at that stage of my career. If you go occasionally, you're not so easy to pick up, it's more of a surprise. And by staying back, you keep your shape and you're more solid as a team. And I had to prove myself to him when he first came which put a block on the goalscoring a little bit as well.

"But once I showed him what I could do, I was off again and those first three seasons back in the top league, I got 50 goals. Goalscoring is always easier if you've got other players getting them as well, and overall that was one of the best spells I had here, especially when Ron wanted me to get forward more. I got all my confidence back after a few lean years, it was just a shame I was at the wrong end of the age scale!

"All I ever wanted to do from the time I first started playing football was score goals, nothing else. Every game I played, that was what I was after. If we won but I hadn't scored, I was pleased for the team but disappointed myself because that was just inbred in me, the need to score goals. I did pick up a lot of records around that time, goals, appearances, but that's because I was a one-club man, I was here a long time, I was pretty lucky with injuries. I loved every minute of representing the Albion and I love being connected with it even now. I never wanted to leave here, I used to enjoy coming in to training, loved playing, it was a marvellous time for me. Big Ron started calling me Mr. Albion! He said they should build a statue of me in the town centre!"

Bomber was, is and always will be a West Brom legend, and his club captain at the time, John Wile, is unstinting in his praise. "I saw a lot of good players at the club down the years, but I've never seen anyone with such incredible accuracy with a shot as Bomber. In training and matches, he worked at getting the ball on target and making the goalkeeper work, and he would do that the vast majority of the time. A good, clean striker of the ball, great power and good anticipation too. He had good pace, great engine, and if the ball was in the slot for him, he could hit it like nobody else. Above all, he had a fantastic appetite for the game. When John Giles came in and then Ron Atkinson, they got him doing what he was best at again, and that was great for everybody, Tony and the team. He had an incredible sense for a goal, the knack of being in the right place at the right time, the goalscorer's instinct."

Bomber passed that knack down the Albion generations too, to a young man who, while not quite his equal as a goalscorer, did make a reputation for himself as possibly the greatest player ever to wear the stripes, 26 England goals in 90 games making Bryan Robson a true legend of the game.

"Goalscoring really came fairly naturally to me to be honest. When I ran forward from midfield, it was just a natural progression that was in my game, and nobody coached that into me, I just seemed to be able to arrive in the box at the right time to get on the end of things, which was a bit like Tony Brown in some ways. Tony was one of the best midfield players ever as far as scoring goals was concerned; he was incredible. He was a great striker of the ball. He was a little bit different to me, probably more of a forward, and he was an absolute top-class striker of the ball where I probably never scored the great goals that he did, but we were similar in that we'd make runs from deep, and that makes it hard for defenders to pick you up, so you can create chances like that. You couldn't fail to learn from watching him."

European competition came around again next, but Albion's trip out to Portugal was nothing like as taxing as the Turkish trials, and Sporting Braga – a club that would later sell Jordao to the Albion – were brushed aside by two goals without reply, Cyrille Regis adding to his burgeoning reputation with two goals inside a minute. Suddenly those two reverses at the start of the month looked no more than a blip and Albion were on the march again, an impression reinforced on October 21st when Coventry City were on the receiving end of an emphatic beating, 7-1, a result all the more impressive given Coventry's solid start to the season, which saw them go into the game just a point behind Albion, having conceded only ten goals in ten games. Not that that cut much ice with the Baggies according to Ron Atkinson, who says, "We loved playing Coventry, we always got goals against them, and at the time I remember saying I'd got their manager Gordon Milne at home on my mantelpiece because we'd beat them that often!"

Tony Brown also felt there was no chance of another European hangover. "Whenever we saw Coventry were coming up, we were all ready for it because they were a side that we invariably did well against, and we often gave them a proper lacing! They were one of those sides that you have the Indian sign over, you never think you'll have any trouble with them. We used to go out knowing we'd get plenty of goals against them, and on that particular day, they deserved everything that was coming to them because they wore the worst kit of all time! That chocolate-brown thing with the big T insignia on it, it was horrible – when we saw them wearing that in the tunnel we couldn't work out what they'd got on. Awful, the most horrible kit I ever saw!"

35

"We just couldn't stop scoring against them, we massacred them; Len Cantello got the first, I scored, Cyrille and Laurie got a couple each, even Derek Statham got up and knocked one in as well – what a player he was! That was why that side was, for me, just that bit better than the one in the 1960s, because we got so many goals. In the 1960s we won things, the FA Cup, and that makes it special in itself, but that '70s team was just so exciting to be a part of; it was like everything just came together at once, every player was a class player. We threw men forward from all over the pitch and it was just a pleasure to be in a team that wanted to go forward, and it was that that set me on the way to the goalscoring record here. It's not often that you go out week after week expecting to win every game, fearing nobody and expecting to play well into the bargain. It was a terrific side, back to front."

A hard-won point was collected at Maine Road in a 2-2 draw with Manchester City, former favourite Asa Hartford snatching one of City's goals, Regis and Robson ensuring the Baggies didn't go home empty-handed, a vital point as it turned out for, on Merseyside, Liverpool were suffering their first defeat of the season, 1-0 at Goodison Park, a result that brought Everton to within two points of their red neighbours, Albion three points further behind.

The following Wednesday the Braga job was finished in muted fashion, though the 1-0 scoreline gave blessed relief to Alistair Brown. The man who finished the season as top scorer was on target to register his first goal in nearly ten weeks, a simple poacher's goal from close range, an important one in the context of the season, as he admits. "Ron had said I was going to be the first choice up front with Cyrille and we didn't have much back up, but when you're not scoring, your confidence goes and you start snatching at things."

Despite the barren spell, his team-mates recognised Ally's contribution to the side, namesake Tony saying, "He never got the praise he should have because everybody raved about Cyrille, but Ally was an important member of that team, a vital player for us. It was a pleasure to play with him as well because off the pitch he was a great character in the dressing room. Always got a fag in his hand, box of fags with him wherever he went. A prankster, one of the lads, everybody took his jokes in the right spirit, and he was important in creating the right atmosphere. Liked his golf as well, still does. But not as much as his fags though!

"On the pitch, he never stopped, he was all action, always running about. He had an up-and-down career here, a few barren spells, but he was a good player for us, led the line really well, and always chipped in with goals. Ally did the donkey work up front, the chasing, the running down the channels, the grafting, and that was great for Cyrille especially because Cyrille never had the greatest stamina in the world. Cyrille was the man for exploding over short distances, but Ally was the long distance man who'd run defenders down."

Regis is also full of praise for the man forced to operate in his gigantic shadow. "Ally Brown was great for me to play alongside. Totally unselfish player, did loads of running for the team and scored bagloads of goals for us as well, 24 by the end of that season. We had a good balance, he knew the game, scored some terrific goals. I had that pace, he had that maturity, I was inexperienced, a bit raw. Ron Atkinson gave him a new lease of life. Ronnie Allen didn't maybe believe in him but Ron filled him with confidence, and the chemistry was just right between the two of us. He didn't get the

praise mediawise like some of us did but he was every bit as important as anyone in that team."
Modest under the weight of those accolades, Ally recalls that, "In one of the papers the one day, the headline was "Ally is Albion's Action Man!" And that stuck for a long time. Brendon Batson still calls me Action now! I probably did a fair bit of the grafting, and it worked especially well with Cyrille Regis. Once he got going, people looked at Cyrille as the main threat, he was the main target for our defenders and midfielders; I ran off him a lot and we just seemed to click."

With the Action Man back among the goals, Albion were on the up again, crucial going into a November period that would see them face both Second City sides in derby games at The Hawthorns and make the journey out to Spain to take on Valencia and the man who won the 1978 World Cup, the most exciting, charismatic footballer on earth - Mario Kempes.

CHAPTER SIX

SHOW ME A HERO AND I'LL WRITE YOU A TRAGEDY

It wasn't all champagne football back in 1978, and if you think that "1-0 to the Albion" was a scoreline that the club only discovered under Gary Megson, you're wrong. November saw the Baggies reel off three of them in a row, the first coming at home to Birmingham City. Blues were rooted to the foot of the First Division, and with their hierarchy coming to accept that Trevor Francis' days at St Andrews were numbered as Division Two beckoned, manager Jim Smith invested in the man he hoped would be Trevor's eventual replacement, Alan Buckley. But where Buckley had been a free-scoring forward in the lower echelons of the Football League with Walsall, in the top flight he looked totally out of his depth – using him to succeed the brilliant Francis was like replacing Shergar with Muffin the Mule. He never got a sniff of a goal at The Hawthorns, and though Albion stuttered, they did enough to get a winner when John Trewick scored from long range.

Trewick was very much the utility man of the team, filling in for injuries when the chance arose, but he was no mere reserve. Cast in the Giles mould, a devotee of passing football, one for whom possession was all, he was a valuable member of what really was a twelve-man team, following in the footsteps of Bryan Robson who had previously done the all-rounder's job. "I played in lots of different positions for the team, left-back, midfield, centre half, centre forward and I loved that variety early on. Looking back, there's no doubt that it made me a better player. Playing in those different roles, you learn to appreciate what your team-mates do and what they need in different areas of the pitch, and so because I did get all over the place, you learn things, pick it up from games, and you just have a better overall understanding of the game. I think the same was true of John Trewick."

John Wile is also full of praise for Trewick, saying, "John was very important. He didn't play all the games, but he'd come in when he got the chance, played well every time, always completely reliable, and he helped keep people on their toes. Everybody who knows John will tell you he's not short of an opinion, and he's happy to give it you! He was a strong character, but you had to be to survive in that side. He came down from the North east as a schoolboy in the holidays, and he played centre forward to start with. In practice matches I'd play against him, and he was an aggravating little so-and-so! He was a good player, he admired Johnny Giles, played the game that way, and he was very unlucky to come through at a time when we had so many good people in midfield, like Len, Bomber, Bryan. It was tough to get in and get established, and like Len and Bryan before him, he played a lot of different positions because Ron trusted him to fill in."

As Wile avers, Trewick never has been scared to make a point when he needs to, an attribute which has made him an outstanding coach since he hung up his boots. "If I think something needs to be said, I'll not shy away from saying it. In football you've a duty to do that, whichever side of the fence you're on, but it doesn't always make you popular!" In spite of that, John was a key component, a good player for the cause and someone who always had Albion's best interests at heart, whether as player, community officer or coach. As a player, in the long term, perhaps his devotion to the patient game counted against him as Atkinson looked to up the tempo, but at least November saw him getting a run in the side, initially as replacement for Derek Statham, then Tony Brown, and it was Trewick who set up Ally Brown to earn Albion's second 1-0 win in a row at Portman Road.

Albion's paper-thin squad was stretched further still with injury to Cyrille Regis before the Bolton game, but Action Man Ally was the man on the spot to give Albion another crucial win as the side slowly started to close the gap at the top. Not that a lack of players was really an issue for manager Atkinson. "You didn't operate on big squads in those days, not even Liverpool, and consequently we more or less played the same side week in, week out. But saying that, nobody could get past the players who'd got the shirts because they were very good players playing consistently at their peak. We might not have had the biggest squad in the world but we didn't have many weaknesses!"

The win at Burnden Park meant Albion had won five out of six since the Tottenham defeat at the start of October, Albion going past Forest – still unbeaten but with nine draws from 15 starts – into third place, four points behind Liverpool. It was an encouraging position from which to embark on possibly the toughest game in Albion's history.

The reward for overcoming Sporting Braga was a third-round meeting with the favourites for the competition, Valencia of Spain. That they were so installed was largely down to one man, Mario Kempes, who had finished the previous summer's World Cup tournament as top scorer and the biggest single reason why Argentina carried off FIFA's trophy in their own back yard. Kempes was strong, muscular, willing to mix it with defenders, lightning quick when running onto or with the ball and with a striker's uncanny knack for putting the ball in the back of the net. At that time, he was the hottest name in world football, the Maradona or the Ronaldo of his era. And Albion were coming up against not just him, but one of the midfield stars of that Mundial, West Germany's elegant Rainer Bohnhof, now plying his trade in the UK as the coach of Scotland's Under-21 side.

These were two genuine stars of the world stage, huge personalities and the kind of player that, way back when, you could hardly imagine taking on the Baggies. OK, Albion's UEFA Cup run was bound to end, but what a way to go, as Tony Brown concedes. "Perhaps youngsters don't quite understand how big a thing it was to play them. But six months earlier, Mario Kempes had won Argentina the World Cup pretty much on his own, he scored twice in the World Cup Final – it'd be like having Ronaldo come to play against us now. Bohnhof was a marvellous player as well, he'd probably have got in the midfield of any world team at the time. Some of the Spanish players were handy as well! They were a spectacular team, and when we got drawn against them, everybody thought that was our UEFA Cup finished with because everybody expected them to win the competition."

And yet, and yet. Confidence was so high in the Albion camp that they flew out to Spain in the genuine belief that Valencia were not invincible, that if they could find their very best form, Kempes and his mates would quickly find out they were in a real game. Ron Atkinson certainly relished the chance, and recalls, "That night in Valencia was a special one, really memorable. They had a side that was probably as good as anything in the world at that point. But when we went abroad for European games, we used to treat them as something to be enjoyed, something where the pressure was off a bit. So we just enjoyed going to these new cities, new grounds, coming across these great players; we just looked on it as something a bit different. A change is as good as a rest if you like."

Equally, striking a blow against the Spaniards would simultaneously deliver a blow to the heart of English football. For all Albion's cavalier play and their impressive results, for all that here we had a side that had been gradually building to a peak over very nearly four years, few at home took them seriously. In their typically patronising fashion, the national media dismissed the Albion as a flash in the pan, no real threat to the likes of Liverpool and Cloughie's Nottingham Forest, nothing more than a sideshow that would crumble when the competition was at its fiercest. What West Brom needed was a special win against a special side to ram that criticism back down their throats. Valencia offered that momentous opportunity for the team to come of age.

According to John Wile, the side was ready for it. "It was tremendously exciting to think who we were taking on. We'd had Valencia watched, and of course we'd seen some of them in the World Cup. To think we were out to stop Kempes playing! I remember being nervous before the game. Confident, but nervous. We went out there and got pelted with oranges and tangerines as we ran out, but we didn't worry about it and put in a great performance from back to front. We were good at closing people down, and as soon as he got it, all the good lessons we'd learned under Don Howe and John Giles came through. We closed him down but we didn't get too close because Kempes used to like that, because he'd just roll round you and be away. He was a big fella, very strong, so you had to stand up to him. We used to test people's courage out early on, we'd see if they were up for it, and we had one or two who could do it, but Kempes kept coming, to be fair to him. A great left foot, looked the part as well with his long hair, but we just set about denying him the space to play in, frustrated him and it worked. We gradually got on top, played our game, let them know they weren't going to get anything for nothing!"

For all their confidence, Albion were down inside 14 minutes when Felman headed in, but that was to be no more than the warm-up act for the main performer. This was the night when Laurie Cunningham joined football's immortals while ironically, tragically, setting in train the sequence of events that would lead to his dreadfully premature death in Spain just a decade later. This was the night when Laurie Cunningham proved that, at his best, he could put a World Cup winner in the shade, could produce a kind of performance that could only come from the Gods, 90 minutes touched by the rarest genius as Tony Brown agrees.

"I was injured for the first leg out in Spain, and I watched it from up in the stands. It was crazy, the atmosphere was unlike anything else I've ever seen. But everyone will tell you that, that night, Laurie Cunningham was just out of this world, stole the show. I've never seen a performance like it; it was unbelievable. He ran the full back ragged every time he got the ball. In the finish, the Valencia crowd were throwing oranges at him, trying to upset him and slow him down, they were that annoyed with him because he was turning them inside out, giving them a right roasting. He scored the equaliser, and we drew 1-1. That night got him noticed in Spain and got him the move to Real Madrid in the summer and, because of that, ironically the success that night was the beginning of the end for that team. But it was magic while it lasted." Wile agrees that Cunningham was extraordinary, but adds, "To be fair, I don't know why Real Madrid didn't buy us all because we were all brilliant that night!"

Watching him at the closest of quarters was Albion right-back Brendon Batson, who was often the water carrier for Cunningham, fetching the ball, delivering it to him so that he could go off on a flight of fancy. "Laurie was an extraordinary talent, a great athlete, he had wonderful balance. He was superb even under pressure, and supporters saw plenty of examples of that, especially in the game where he sold himself to Real Madrid, when we drew in Valencia. He was very supple, quite balletic and graceful in his movement and such an exciting player to watch. I always used to thank Him upstairs that I didn't have to mark him in that game in Valencia because the poor guy out there must have had the worst night of his life trying to stop him!"

Nobody else moved like Laurie. He covered the turf with an effortless grace, gliding across the ploughed fields that made up most of the grounds of England at that time – quite what he'd be able to do on the bowling greens we play on now is anyone's guess. It was all to do with balance, a tremendous turn of pace and an endearing arrogance – Laurie knew just how good he was, and, unlike many, he wasn't afraid to go out and try to prove it on every occasion he put on the Albion shirt. Yet for all that extrovert quality on the pitch, off it he was a very different character according to Batson.

"He was quite an introvert off the pitch, and he needed people around him, which was why he kept going back down to London because that's where his roots were. Maybe a year more in the spotlight here would have been good for him, because the fame didn't rest too comfortably with him and he got much more of it at Madrid. But I wouldn't have liked to have had to make that choice, because who knows if those opportunities will ever come round again."

Laurie could never have been a white footballer or, more accurately, no white footballer could ever have been Laurie Cunningham. He was Funkadelic, he was Shaft, he was Robert Johnson, he was Malcolm X, he was cool, he moved to his own rhythm, lithe, athletic, a footballer rooted in jazz, its music and dance. When he first signed for Albion I remember watching aghast as he appeared on the TV show *Magpie* to tell Mick Robertson – or was it Brian May? – that he took regular dance classes to help his movement, this in an era when any lad expressing an interest in such things could expect to be stoned to death in the playground.

Being dismissed as effete and effeminate was of course the least of Laurie's worries in an era when opposition fans wanted to rip him to pieces for the heinous crime of being black – nobody who was there will ever forget the chilling sound of Wolves fans drumming against the corrugated sheets at the back of the Smethwick End, chanting, "Pull the trigger, shoot the nigger," every time Laurie got the ball. Understandably, he found it hard to cope initially, though the later arrival of Regis and Batson gave him a surrogate family who helped share the burden, but time after time, he reacted in the way that he knew best. He proved that this black man was the most exciting footballer in the country, winning over some hearts and minds in the process, driving the remainder, the card-carrying, sheet-wearing KKKretins apoplectic with rage as he tore their Aryan side – itself often sporting at least one or two black players by this time, though the stupidity of these supporters also often extended to selective colour blindness – to shreds.

Having had the privilege of watching Cunningham's all-too-brief Albion career at close quarters, I can't say I've ever seen a player to match him at his best, while as John Trewick avers, "If you thought he was good in games, you should have seen what he could do in training!" Cyrille Regis' suggestion that Thierry Henry is the closest in the modern game makes sense, and as Laurie's closest colleague in the game, who can argue with him? But footballing comparisons seem invidious when dealing with such a genuine one-off. Perhaps the closest parallels you can draw are with jazz greats, men like John Coltrane and, especially, Miles Davis.

42

Like Miles, Cunningham was feeling his way towards a goal, a performance, a greatness that he couldn't prove existed, but which he sensed was out there somewhere. Riffing, exploring, pushing the boundaries, feeling his way, then suddenly, from seemingly nowhere, the experimentation would coalesce, producing magic, hitting the lost chord, finding the melody, creating moments the rest of us couldn't even dream about, so original were they. Always questing, searching, it had its downside, the days when the muse wasn't there, which meant he never captured the consistency of Willie Johnston or Clive Clark for instance, all of which could make him exasperating – I vividly recall the previous season, at home to Leicester, when faced with a gaping net from five yards out, in an effort to make a tap-in aesthetically pleasing, he contrived to side-foot the ball wide. Yet when the Gods smiled on him, when the essence was coursing through his veins, he was untouchable, awesome. That night in Valencia was his "Bitches Brew", he'd tapped into something extraordinary, bigger than the man himself, a moment at once exhilarating and, perhaps, frightening. Few, be they musicians, writers, sportsmen, whoever, can tame those flames of genius, can bend them to their will, can fail to be consumed by them – Best and Gascoigne give ample evidence of that. Ultimately, albeit in different ways, Laurie's gifts, their capricious nature and the envy they invoked, would exact their revenge on him.

But for the moment, Cunningham was an irresistible force, as Tony Brown recalls. "He was so gifted, lightning pace. People say players have pace without thinking these days, but it's what you do with it that counts. If all you needed was pace, you'd get Linford Christie playing for England wouldn't you? He had pace and incredible ball control at the same time. Laurie got goals, a good header of the ball, perfect balance, hard to get the ball off him, kept control of it well. He was a genuinely world-class player and should have got a lot more recognition than he did."

43

Fittingly he was the instigator of Albion's goal in the only game played between the two Valencia ties, setting up Batson to win Albion's penalty in the 1-1 draw with Aston Villa. But even the big local derby paled into insignificance in the face of the impending second leg, which stood intriguingly poised at 1-1, the Baggies having the slight advantage of the away goal.

It's no exaggeration to say that this was one of the most eagerly awaited games ever played at The Hawthorns, and those who have grown up knowing only the Premiership era, the satellite television age, will find it impossible to imagine just how exciting it was to have Valencia in town. These, remember, were the days when the only domestic game that was shown live on television was the FA Cup Final. Occasional England matches got the same treatment – usually the annual punch-up with the Scots and maybe a crucial World Cup qualifier – and then you had World Cup games, but there was nothing like the saturation coverage you get today. Even European Cup matches, except for the final itself, were relegated to highlights packages late at night on *Sportsnight With Coleman* and the like. And the idea that you could watch Serie A or La Liga live on TV every week was so bizarre as to not even be worth thinking about.

Added to that was the fact that the First Division was very much an English league – the most exotic foreigners on show came from Scotland, Wales, Northern or Southern Ireland, and it wasn't until Ricky Villa and Ossie Ardiles pitched up at Tottingham in the aftermath of the 1978 World Cup that the Football League began to really open its doors to international interlopers, so the opportunity to see any foreign side was a chance you had to take, particularly in the light of Albion's poor record at qualifying for Europe in the past. And getting to see Kempes as well; that was the icing on the cake. So much so that the evening before the game, when Valencia trained under the lights at The Hawthorns, dozens of fans braved the arctic conditions – the first hint of the bitter winter that was to come to stand in Halfords Lane just to watch him get on the team bus, and get the great man's autograph – I've still got it.

The following evening was just one of those magical nights of football that you take to the grave with you, unforgettable, spine-tingling, enthralling stuff, and all played in freezing cold under the floodlights, the perfect ingredients for an electric atmosphere. With the old ground crammed to capacity, John Wile admits that, "Those two games against Valencia are probably my two favourite games from my career. Evening games and European games are always special, playing against a top side, playing the football we played; it was a great spectacle."

Tony Brown had missed the match out in Spain, but there was never any danger of him missing the return, and just as well, for he was Albion's match winner, scoring both goals in a barely believable 2-0 win as the Baggies were simply too good for them, the passionate support playing its part in a result that reverberated around the continent, as Bomber recalls. "If the atmosphere was amazing in Spain, it was incredible here as well, such a night, I'll never forget it; you really could cut it with a knife, absolutely electric. We still had plenty to do, it was all to play for and we loved those sorts of games, especially night matches, we used to excel in them for some reason. I scored a penalty to start things off, but the second was a goal I'll always remember, it's in my top half-dozen. Laurie made a great run down the right, crossed it in, and I just caught it smack on the volley and it rattled into the corner and the whole place went berserk.

"We thoroughly deserved to beat them, and I think people knew then that we were a top side. It'd be like beating Juventus or Milan or Real Madrid today because Valencia were that good. Perhaps you don't get the same excitement from European games now because there are so many Champions League games and such a lot on the telly, but to see Kempes in the flesh was out of this world then, to have players like him at The Hawthorns, it was a real thrill for supporters. And to give them a good beating, well, everybody knew we were something to be reckoned with then."

CHAPTER SEVEN

MIGHTY LIKE A ROSE

A solitary month doesn't make a season, but if West Bromwich Albion has ever enjoyed a month more than December 1978, you'd be hard pushed to name it. If ever the club and its team sent out a message to the rest of the country and the rest of Europe that they were in the presence of something undeniably special, then it was during a period when we tore the First Division to shreds, and all in the wake of that legendary UEFA Cup victory over Valencia.

With Mario Kempes and his colleagues sent packing and Albion enjoying a three-month hiatus from European competition before the quarter-final tie against Red Star Belgrade, it was time for the club to turn its attention to domestic matters once more and the first genuinely sustained assault on the First Division title since 1953/54. The month dawned with Albion in third place, six points behind Liverpool but with a game in hand. It ended with them still in third place, but with the deficit clawed back to just two points, that precious game still in hand – win it, and the Baggies would be joint top.

It was an extraordinary month, yet one which looked anything but promising as Albion fans assessed the fixtures ahead, with trips to Wolves, Arsenal and Manchester United in the offing. But before that, Albion's first game after Valencia was a home game against mid-table Middlesbrough. In retrospect it was perhaps the ideal fixture. Had they played a top-of-the-table side, reaching another peak within 72 hours of disposing of the Spanish giants might have been too much to ask, whereas had they been pitted against one of the real basement sides, it could easily have been a case of "after the Lord Mayor's show", Albion losing concentration and dropping valuable points. But a game against John Neal's workmanlike outfit meant the Baggies coming up against a side they knew they had to take seriously and one which they'd need to be at their best to overcome. With the crowd suffering football fatigue – only 19,949 turned up compared with the 35,118 who'd seen Valencia vanquished – there were no such failings on the field, and Albion swept to a 2-0 win courtesy of goals from Cyrille Regis and Len Cantello.

That set up a trip to Molineux to take on a Wolves team that was playing without form or confidence, rooted in the bottom three with thirteen defeats from eighteen games. With Albion hitting their stride and Wolves going backwards, this was one derby game where the form book didn't go out of the window, and Albion cruised to a 3-0 win, Tony Brown scoring a real cracker to set up the victory.

"To go out and win 3-0 at their place was a fabulous result, especially coming off the back of the win against Valencia ten days before and then beating Middlesbrough at home on the Saturday. It was a terrific game, a terrific atmosphere, and it wasn't as one sided as the score suggests, because we had to play well to beat them. Steve Daley had some good chances in that game for them as well, and Tony Godden had to make some super saves. Tony was always a bit underrated at the time because that was the era of Clemence and Shilton, who were out of this world, but Tony was a good 'keeper. He made some terrific stops and right the way through his time for us his reflexes were tremendous, he was as good as anybody at that, to be honest. And that afternoon at the Molineux he used them to good effect because Daley would have had a couple of goals if it hadn't been for Tony. But we played well that day as well, because we were just running into a period where we were right at the peak of our form, game after game after game. You have to cherish spells like that because, however good the team you're in, periods like that when everything comes off don't come around very often."

Bomber's strike was, like his goal at Chelsea, another case of him being too darned quick for the TV cameras to react and catch it properly. Fortunately, his memory of it is still crystal clear.

"I can remember the goal, it's flashing in front of my eyes now as I talk about it! It was another one from about 30 yards if I remember right, another one that the camera never caught; you only see it going in the net! I made one as well for Ally Brown, went into the box, just nicked it to the one side for Ally to get in and finish it off.

"So that was a terrific Saturday afternoon for everybody involved at the club because it's always special to beat your local rivals. For the supporters it never gets much better than going to Molineux and winning! To be honest, the Wolves don't really bother me that much, I'd always rather beat the Villa than the Wolves because, when I first got to the Albion, it was always drummed into me that the Villa were the team we had to beat; they were the biggest rivals, so I've always tended to get more satisfaction from turning them over. But to beat any local rival is always a big result for the fans.

"The one thing I will say about Wolves in those days was that you always got a brilliant atmosphere at the old Molineux, which you just don't get nowadays since they've redeveloped the stadium, impressive though the new ground is. I think it's something to do with the fact that the corners aren't filled in there, and you do lose some of the intensity when the stadium doesn't wrap itself round and enclose everybody; you just lose that little bit of something, which is why I'm pleased that The Hawthorns pretty much wraps right the way round. And of course, you used to get nearly twice as many people in there, which makes a bit of a difference! I played there in front of 52,000 people at the start of my career, and it was just white-hot in the place, unbelievable atmosphere to play in. That was at the start of the 1967 season and from memory, I think that was the night when I punched one in, like Maradona I've only recently admitted to that one! But the place on that night was just unbelievable, a tight little ground, supporters right on top of you, fantastic theatre to play football in. Going back to the 3-0 game, that showed that we were gaining consistency, that we were going to be a threat right through to the death that season. And that turned out to be the last game that we played before Christmas so it wasn't a bad little present for the supporters!" With Liverpool losing at Bristol City that day and Everton dropping a point at home to Leeds, it was a super Saturday for Albion.

Albion were snowed off the following week, a game against Southampton victim of the weather, but while the Baggies got in a bit of extra Christmas shopping, their next opponents, Arsenal, drew level on points by hammering Tottenham 5-0 in the north London derby game, adding extra spice to what was already a huge Boxing Day game. Ron Atkinson remembers it with some relish. "They'd been brilliant against Spurs; it was the Liam Brady show and he scored an incredible goal for them, bending it in from the edge of the box. He was in great form that year, a lovely player. But we genuinely weren't bothered by the opposition, so we went down to Highbury, gave them a real pounding early on and finished up winning 2-1, which was one of the best results we got all season."

Tony Brown is less dewy-eyed at the memory of that game. In fact he barely remembers it at all – he didn't get on the scoresheet after all! "I know we won 2-1, but to be honest, I really don't remember very much about the game, which is funny because it was a great win for us. We had an absolutely awful record down there at Highbury, even when we were playing in semi finals! It was a bogey ground for us, we couldn't ever get anything to bring back from there, so to go and beat them down in north London just showed how well we were playing at the time, even though Arsenal weren't quite the great side they had been at the start of the 1970s or that they've since become again. Saying that, it still took something special to beat them on their own patch. But none of it has stuck in my mind, which is odd."

Goals from Robson and Ally Brown won that one, but on reflection, it's probably no surprise that Bomber has blotted that one out because something yet more exciting was just around the corner.

"I suppose the thing is that we then went to Old Trafford a few days after the Arsenal match and were involved in that 5-3 game. That sort of overshadowed everything around it, and when you look back on that season, you tend just to dwell on that one instead of a few of the others. It was only four days later, which made for a pretty tough Christmas period – Arsenal and Manchester United, both away, in the space of four days! Christmas and Easter are always very big periods that sometimes make or break a season, and we just had a cracking Christmas that year.

"The United game was one of the most exciting I played in, end to end, both sides totally committed to attacking. But we played some incredible football that day, especially when you think we came from behind to win. That's always special, but especially away from home, and even more so at Old Trafford because United were my team when I was growing up.

"Everybody went overboard on the United game a little bit because it was such an incredible game that had just about everything in it. There was some scintillating football played that day; it really was a classic, and even now when I go to supporters, club meetings, that's the one that always comes up, everybody raves about it. And we could have had eight to be honest because Gary Bailey made some unbelievable saves for them. Two from Cyrille were just out of this world, then Pop Robson had a great chance when he ran through the middle and I knocked one into him from the right-hand side. He was clear in the box, but Bailey spread himself and made another top save. Tony made a couple of good stops for us as well, but most of the chances were coming at United's end!"

United were first to register, Brian Greenhoff setting the standard with a cracker from the edge of the box. It didn't take Albion long to get back on terms, Bomber knocking one in in front of the Stretford End after receiving a lovely ball from Cunningham, and an historic goal it was too. "Bailey was outstanding, but at least I scored past him, which made a bit of history, funnily enough. I didn't realise it until recently, but somebody told me that I'm the only player to have played and scored against a father and a son as goalkeepers. When I made my debut at Ipswich, Gary's dad Roy was in goal for them and I scored past him, and then I scored past Gary about fifteen years later! Apparently nobody else has managed to score past a father and son!"

Albion's second was no less historic, if in a different way, Len Cantello scoring a rasping drive from 25 yards to win ITV's "Goal of the Season" prize. The goal started with the rampant Laurie Cunningham, as Brendon Batson recalls. "His close control was incredible. I've seen a clip of Len Cantello's goal put to music, and it starts with Laurie out on the left on the halfway line. He literally starts to waltz across the pitch, goes past a number of challenges until he's about 10 yards outside

47

the box before passing to Cyrille, and Cyrille back heels it to Len to smack it in. But you watch it in slow motion and look at how many times people try to knock him off the ball, foul him, but he rides them, keeps tight control of the ball, he's incredible. The goal would never have come about if Laurie had broken down at any time, but his movement right across the pitch set it all up."

United were back on terms when McQueen bulleted a header in, and an eleven-minute scoring spree ended with its fifth goal, United nosing in front again with another cracking goal, Sammy McIlroy dancing into the box before slashing the ball across Godden and in.

That wasn't quite it for the first half though, Bomber grabbing his second in the 45th minute just as the teams were preparing for the half-time cuppa, a warming brew that was much needed given the freezing temperatures the match was played in. The Albion manager had obviously nipped off a bit early to put the kettle on, as Tony remembers.

"I equalised right on the stroke of half-time and I don't think there was even time for United to kick off again, but while that was going on, Big Ron was on his way to the dressing room. We walked in and Ron started his team talk.

"Doing great lads, doing great. Keep playing like that and you'll get the equaliser, no danger."

"So one of the lads said, "What do you mean boss, Bomber's just scored! We're level!"

"We never are! I've missed that coming down to the dressing room! Was it a good goal? Right. Keep playing like that and you'll get the winner, no danger!"

"We were in hysterics in the dressing room, and I'm sure that helped the way we approached the second half, and the way we approached most games really, with a smile on our faces, playing good football. And we did, we went back out there, tore into them and won 5-3."

Victory was completed with a second-half annihilation of Dave Sexton's side, only Gary Bailey's heroics keeping United in the game with save after brilliant save. Route one was the way to goal four, Regis heading on a Godden goal kick to Cunningham, who showed stunning acceleration and poise to hurtle past the defence and score with a precise finish. With time ebbing away, there was still a chance for Albion to apply the *coup de grace*. Neither of their twin strikers had yet found the net until Ally Brown fed Regis in the inside right channel, Cyrille slamming the ball past Bailey with venom borne from the frustration of the United 'keeper denying him acrobatically on at least two occasions. But like Cunningham, when the mood took him, Regis was an irresistible force, as John Wile says.

"Jeff was always the idol here, he always will be the King, and he was an incredible player, terrific centre forward. And we hadn't replaced him. Then Cyrille came in and it was pure, raw talent. He came in at the start of the 1977/78 season and we used to play practice games, reserves against the first team, and we'd treat them pretty seriously, play properly, though with a view to not getting injured. So I came up against Cyrille for the first time and somebody stuck the ball in the box and I thought to myself, "I'll head that away because I've headed 99 of them away in these games, I'll get this one as well!" Suddenly, there's this guy coming over the top and he got there before me. So I thought, "Right. I'll have a go for the next one!" So I did, and he still got there first, and then you start thinking, "He's got something about him!"

"He got in the team soon after, scored a couple in his first game and he was away. It says a lot about coaching that there was this raw talent there, hadn't had the rough edges knocked off him, but he was unstoppable. All he knew was, when he got the ball, he wanted to go for goal and shoot. He was electrifying, and I guess it was the beauty of innocence really. He was so refreshing in his style, nothing cynical. If he kicked you it was an accident; if you got hold of him he'd shrug you off. He said he didn't work out, it was just a natural physique he had, and a natural talent to go with it. So quick, strong, a great striker of the ball, direct. As a defender, the last thing you want is somebody running at you with pace because you don't have many choices – you either back off or try to go in and win it. He'd run at you, and he'd terrify defenders with his pace and his power. He still goes on now about how I'd knock the ball up to him – "It'd be up in the air, I'd have to catch it on my neck!" He's one of life's genuinely nice people and he deserves to be held in the awe and respect that he is by Albion fans because he's a smashing guy."

Bomber is equally effusive about a man who genuinely helped change the face of English football. "When he was in full flight, he was frightening. I'm glad he was on our side because if you had him going full pelt bearing down on you, you were going to be in some trouble. He was massive, and he always used to play it up by having a very tight shirt on so that you could see his muscles!

"He was great over short distances, tremendous pace, but further than 30 or 40 yards and he was hopeless! He got real stick in training because if we had a longer run, he was always last. But in football, especially for a goalscorer, it's the first five yards that count, and over that, he was electric. Put the ball in front of him over a few yards and he was incredible.

"He was lucky to have some experience around him early on, myself, Willie Johnston and Ally Brown as well; I think we helped him a lot. Ally was a great partner for him, very underestimated, a good player in his own right, and he helped get the best out of Cyrille. Ally made great runs, led the line, would never stop running, worked the channels, told Cyrille where to go, where to play the ball, and that was a big part of his development."

Typical of the man, Regis would rather talk about the team than himself. And his analysis of why that Albion side was so special is right on the money.

"The prerequisite of any good side is intelligence, the ability to make the right decisions quickly on the ball, the mental strength to keep going when you need to and a winning mentality. You need good tactics, the right kind of leadership; all those things need to go together with talent before you can put a really useful team out on the field. I suppose there is a formula because the likes of Liverpool, Manchester United and Arsenal have been successful over sustained periods, but it takes some doing. But when it does click, it's something special, and that was what we had here.

"It was a question of timing I think. The blend was good, plenty of experience, but then you had the younger players who were maturing, starting to step up a gear, people like myself, Derek

Statham, Bryan Robson, Laurie Cunningham, John Trewick, who all now had a year or two of games behind us, had gone beyond the promising youngster stage and were now ready to deliver every week. Stick that with the likes of Tony Brown, John Wile, Ally Rob, Ally Brown, Len Cantello and it was a perfect mix for us. We all had a lot of mutual respect for each other's ability, and I think you need to have that in any successful side."

The massacre in Manchester put an end to December and to 1978, a memorable twelve months in the history of the Baggies, who seemed set to go from strength to strength in the year ahead according to Tony Brown.

"It was a dream month to be honest, we just murdered everybody. That's what confidence does for you, we didn't fear anybody – Valencia, Arsenal, Manchester United, just bring them on! That was how we felt. We knew that team was good enough to take anybody on, anywhere, any time. We just never felt we were going to get beat, we'd tear teams apart, it wasn't like defensive football, wait for them to lose it; it was going at them and putting them under pressure for long, long spells. Teams couldn't get out against us and we made teams pay when we had them under the cosh.

"We scored from all over the park, shared them out which makes it a lot easier – Ally Brown, Cyrille, Laurie, Bryan Robson, myself, five top-class finishers that season, all putting the ball away regularly. You can't go wrong with that as long as you keep them out at the other end, and we had the people at the back to do that. I've already mentioned Tony Godden, but that back four was a bit special, as good as we've ever had here, as good as anything in the world for me at that time. That pairing of John Wile and Ally Robertson were just totally uncompromising they were as solid as rocks. If John Wile didn't get you first off, you knew that Ally Rob would have you, the ball and everything else. Then you had Brendon Batson and Derek Statham, good tacklers, fabulous coming forward, dream players. They're what you need nowadays because they would be superb now, absolutely world class wing-backs, they had the lot."

With a team like that, everything seemed possible for Albion, just two points shy of Liverpool with a game in hand. But the events of December also gave one hint of the one enemy they might not be able to overcome. They'd already had a couple of games postponed by the weather, and with winter closing in, a fixture pile up was one thing Albion didn't need.

50

CHAPTER EIGHT

IN BLACK AND WHITE

Victory in front of the television cameras, by such a remarkable scoreline and with such amazing goals, at Old Trafford put the cap on an astonishing year, an Albion *annus mirabilis*. 1978 saw the club shake off five or six years of decline, of living in the shadows, of being dismissed as a dour Black Country bunch. Albion were looked at in the same swashbuckling light as Kevin Keegan's Newcastle in the mid-1990s, the people's favourites, the side that most neutrals were willing to win the title, to pip Liverpool to the crown, to drag English football from an era of safety first, defensive fodder. Out of darkness came light.

Hand in hand with that mould-breaking football went an upturn in fortunes off the field. Suddenly, you couldn't find a more fashionable side than the Albion. The club was all about glamour, about seizing life and living it, going for glory, all guns blazing and damn the consequences, going out and winning games rather than boring the opposition into losing them, and people warmed to it. A big side needs big characters, and Albion had plenty of them, from the top down. Ron Atkinson loved to play the fame game, and he was carving out his reputation as a Champagne Charlie – even though he barely touched the stuff. There's no doubt that Atkinson loved to see his name in the press, but his motives weren't entirely selfish, for he recognised that, if you are going to be a big club in the future, you have to behave as though you're a big club now. Talk the talk and there's a fair chance that that will help furnish you with the tools you'll need to one day walk the walk.

Sure, Ron loved the limelight, but like his players, he backed it up with bags of ability, as Cyrille Regis underlines. "For Ron this was his big chance in the game. He was still fairly young, but he was full of confidence, and he knew he was coming to take over a team that was already doing the right things. He looked at us, analysed what we'd got, built on it without making too many changes. He just tweaked it a bit, didn't change the tactics significantly but put his own brand on us, gave us an attitude of no fear, let us go out and play and instilled his energy in us. He loved to be entertained, excited by his team, and he put this philosophy into us, "Go out and play, excite me." We had freedom to express ourselves, not to worry about what we were doing. He always said that he could trust that side. He knew that, if we had a bad game, if we'd had a night out early in the week, whatever it was, we could always bounce back. He knew we would always give it our best when we went out on the pitch.

"Ron was great on television and in the papers, always had a good quote for reporters and so they just wanted more and more from him, so they fed off each other. He liked to be at the centre of things, he played the part to the full, the Mr. Bojangles thing with all the jewellery. He loved every minute of it, thrived on it."

More than Ron Atkinson's thirst for publicity, it was the flamboyant Three Degrees that put Albion on the map, though even then, it was the manager who gave them a shove towards fame as Brendon Batson recalls in this affectionate summing up of his erstwhile manager. "Big Ron was never shy in coming forward to publicise himself or the club – probably in that order! – and that culminated in the Three Degrees business where the focus was on me, Laurie and Cyrille. And we could carry it off because we were playing such great football. It all fell in nicely, and it did put this club on the map. The focus was partly because it was the first time a team had three black players playing at the top of English football, but also we played such attractive football – I'd never seen a full back perform like Derek Statham in my life, we had Bryan Robson, it was an exciting side. But Laurie took most attention because of the question of being the first black player to play for England."

Viewed through the prism of history, it's hard to imagine now just how startling it was to see one of England's top teams fielding three black players, and enthralling black players at that – it was the best part of a decade after Laurie Cunningham's Albion debut before Liverpool went out and bought John Barnes for instance. Nowadays, it's more remarkable if a Premiership team doesn't include a rich synthesis of nationalities and skin tones, but back in the 1970s, the Football League was a whitewash, awash with whites. There had been black players throughout the history of the game but they were few and far between, and though the numbers grew through the 1970s, it wasn't until the Three Degrees took the game by the scruff of the neck that many of the moronic myths about the frailties and inabilities of black players – they don't like it up 'em, they disappear when it's cold, haven't got the heart, can't tackle – were rammed down the throats of the immoral majority. Any black player that took to the field in those days was a harder, braver man than any club-wielding centre half, for here was the modern day equivalent of the Christian being hurled to the lions in front of a baying mob. Perhaps a closer analogy would be the slave being hunted down by the lynch mob in the deep south. These were horrible, disfiguring, depressing times for English football, odious attitudes and institutionalized abusiveness prevailing, creating an atmosphere and a mindset that, in hindsight, put us on a path to the disasters of the late 1980s, offering a tragic but apparently inevitable exorcism which offered the chastened game a chance to have a Year Zero and move on. But at what cost?

Cunningham as we've seen, was an astonishing player, graceful, sinuous, balletic, where Regis was elemental, the muscular explosiveness of a heavyweight puncher combined with the pace of an Olympic sprinter. The build of Sol Campbell, the pace of Thierry Henry, the feet of Ryan Giggs. Add to that a temperament that allowed him to go into the bear pits that some of England's stadia once were, as the main focus of the moronic racist hatred espoused by the terminally-stupid right-wing elements who saw football as a recruiting ground for their fascist filth and to smile at those tormentors and then turn on them the one weapon whose fire they could never return – sheer brilliance. Those of us who saw that were truly blessed. We saw it. We saw Cyrille Regis change English football.

When it comes to naming the great and the good, men who have gone beyond the call of duty, who have entered the football industry, lived in it, inhabited it, made it their own and eventually left it a far richer, better place for their contribution, Cyrille Regis doesn't often get a look-in. Which tells you plenty about the people who compile those sorts of lists. Because Cyrille not only turned English football inside out, he helped changed the way this country behaved. He did that, Cyrille and the men who worked alongside him, men like Brendon Batson, Laurie Cunningham, Remi Moses, Bob Hazell, George Berry, Garth Crooks, Viv Anderson, men who made up the first wave of black footballers, men who changed the face of the game.

They talk about putting statues of Bobby Moore and Alf Ramsey up at the new Wembley, because we're a nation that only honours people in death not while they're still around to thank for their efforts. But great though the contribution of Moore and Ramsey was, it's nothing compared with the achievements of those players who had the guts to stare down the cowards in the National Front, to prove by their ability that black footballers were everything their white counterparts were, and, once and for all, give black players their rightful place at the heart of the game, while helping to reduce racism in wider society at the same time. All that after having been working as an electrician on a building site a couple of years earlier. Now that's an achievement.

Looking back on his colleague, Tony Brown says, "He was a delight to play with, just what you want from a target man. He held the line, received the ball well, protected it, strong as you like, defenders couldn't knock him off the ball, meant that players like me could join up from midfield; I'd make late runs and he'd play me in a lot of times, and that's what top strikers do. Defenders would have to double up on him, and then that left space for the rest of us to exploit. And on top of that, once he'd turned a defender and used that pace of his, there was no catching him; they'd bounce off him, it was amazing, and then he was a superb striker of the ball. He'd got the lot for a front man, and how he didn't get more England caps I don't know. Everybody was raving about him, from a team point of view he was perfect, but they wouldn't give him the chance.

"Cyrille did have to play under a lot of pressure when he came into the side, when there was all that "Three Degrees" business. The atmosphere at grounds was horrible at some places and he had to put up with some terrible abuse from the terraces, but he had a great attitude, great temperament for it. Just shrugged it off, never seemed to let it bother him, just got on with the job. He always felt that the best answer was sticking the ball in the net; that was the way to show them they couldn't beat him. He didn't have a chip on his shoulder; he just wanted to be accepted for who he was. Cyrille was a great lad to have around as well, great in the dressing room, superb in there, a genuinely nice bloke. There was a lot of banter in there, lot of mickey taking, nobody took exception to it and that's important, a major plus because team spirit is so important if you're going to go on and succeed."

53

Cyrille remembers that, "We were breaking new ground. We didn't think of making a stand so much as stretching our talent, but on the back of it came this other stuff, being a role model, destroying myths. What you learn is to turn negatives into positives. "You're giving me abuse; I'll score goals past you." That's the way to hurt them. But from a black perspective, West Brom did wonders for the black community. It was radical, really radical. The real explosion started here without a doubt. Once we'd done it, there was never any excuse not to use black players again. If all that racism was on the streets, affecting my family, that would have been a different ball game. But it was confined to the arena and I could handle it.

"It made a difference to this country. To me one of the best things for race relations here has been black footballers playing the game professionally. Unless there's something wrong with you, you have to ask yourself, "How can I be cheering for a black player on my team and then abusing one on the other side? How can I cheer Cyrille and then give George Berry stick?""

That wave of players, along with musicians like Bob Marley, Smokey Robinson, Otis Redding, Jimi Hendrix and Marvin Gaye, made probably the greatest contribution to race relations in this country, an infinitely greater contribution than any number of well-meaning speeches, pamphlets or government initiatives. They tore up Enoch Powell's inane visions of rivers of blood, exposed the racist, shambling ramblings of out-of-touch Nazis for the garbage they were, and showed a new generation that genius was genius wherever it came from. But God, it was a hard slog, and only those men in the middle will know the price they had to pay, the toll it took of them, how much of their potential was left unfulfilled simply because, unlike their white counterparts, they couldn't just concentrate on their football.

Brendon Batson remembers that, "We used to get some awful letters, and we'd pin them on the dressing room wall and use them for motivation. We joked about it at the time, but the most serious one was when Cyrille got a bullet through the post after he'd been picked for England. That really put a more sinister hue on it, but we just ignored it; we were all the same, we pursued what we wanted to do. None of us dwelt on it. You couldn't.

"People forget sometimes that football grounds were very hostile places in the 1970s, and there were times we were pleased that there were fences up to be honest. It's a credit to the black players of that era that, in spite of what went on, on and off the pitch, there was no reaction. When I was at Cambridge, we were coming back from Bradford, and there'd been a National Front rally up there and our coach was in the middle of it, stuck between coaches carrying all these marchers. They saw me on our coach, and they were spitting at me from inside their own coaches. That sums them up, the spit ran down the windows inside their own coach, but they just wanted to get their feelings across.

"You'd go to places like Chelsea and the NF would be outside giving out leaflets, but it didn't deter black players in coming forward in increasing numbers. If we had been intimidated by it, maybe the next generation wouldn't have come through because their parents might have steered them away from it. It seems strange now that it took so long for there to be a national campaign like "Let's Kick Racism", which only started in 1993 thanks to the PFA, twenty years or more after I started playing. Supporters were waiting for an opportunity to distance themselves from that significant minority who wanted to make life intolerable and "Let's Kick Racism" provided that."

In Batson's subsequent career as an administrator, he has continued to help defeat racism in all its forms, and John Wile agrees that it was his thoughtful nature that was crucial in helping the Three Degrees find their way through those dreadful days. "In life, sometimes things just come together and we had that with the Three Degrees. Brendon was important because he was the steadying hand of the three, but they all needed one another. I think at that time, it might have been harder for just one black player to make an impact because they were unpleasant times to say the least, but there was strength in the fact that there were three of them, and in the fact that there was a good team ethic. They were welcome in the club, in the dressing room, by the fans; there were never any problems inside the club. And the three stood out because they were such superb players and exciting as well.

"I think Ron bought Brendon with a view to taking over from me at centre half in the end. That was his proper position, he'd played there for Cambridge, but when Ron came in, he didn't get on with Paddy Mulligan! Brendon was quick, tackled well, he could get forward, everything you need in a full back. And he handled all the Three Degrees stuff well and was a good influence on Laurie in particular who was a bit more aware of the racial aspect of what he was doing. Laurie would react to the supporters who were having a go at him, where Cyrille would just ignore it because he was so laid back. Brendon helped Laurie cope with it I think."

Calling them "The Three Degrees" nowadays seems to diminish them and their achievement, reducing them almost to a cartoon. Never mind Best, Law and Charlton. Batson, Regis and Cunningham deserve to be called a Holy Trinity. Anyone who ever caught a glimpse of Cunningham at his flying best will never forget the experience, because Laurie was a natural-born footballer, a player of supreme grace, balance, poise, wit and intelligence. It's no exaggeration to say that, had fate been kinder to him, the wider public would now be talking about him in the same breath as George Best, just as Albion aficionados already do. That's no idle comparison either, because Cunningham was good enough to be worthy of mention in the same breath as Bestie.

But Laurie was saddled with another burden. Not only was he closely marked by defenders at a time when the two-footed lunge and the tackle from behind were everyday parts of the game, but he was also one of the key trailblazers for black footballers in England, forced to be a figurehead and singled out for special treatment, some of it complimentary, most of it hateful, hurtful and racist.

When the old Throstle Club stood alongside the Rainbow Stand on the Birmingham Road, some morons disfigured the back of it with racist graffiti attacking Laurie Cunningham, graffiti that was only partially painted out, when the only slogan that ever needed painting about him was "Cunningham is a genius". That verminous scrawl, horrible though it was, was a useful reminder, a legacy from days that we must be ever vigilant against. If racism can so close minds and eyes, if racism can prevent people appreciating the full flowering of one of the greatest talents ever seen in an Albion shirt and in the English game, then you cannot doubt that racism is a hateful, powerful force.

Batson was a full back supreme, an artist. Cyrille Regis was incredible too, a centre forward unlike any we'd seen outside the pages of *Roy of the Rovers*. It was with West Bromwich Albion that he spent his prime years pulling on the blue and white shirt simply because he was so good a player. It is the club's great privilege that it was able to play a part in his story, in Cunningham's and Batson's stories. For all the cups Albion have won, there's no prouder boast for the club than that it helped make racism unacceptable in football. Albion owe the Three Degrees an enormous debt. They owe Albion nothing.

CHAPTER NINE

TOP OF THE WORLD

As Albion bade farewell to 1978 and headed into ther centenary year, there was real belief that that milestone would be marked by the collection of at least one trophy as Albion forged ahead in the league, the UEFA Cup and readied themselves to start the FA Cup campaign with a trip to Highfield Road at the beginning of January. But before they set off in the hunt for a sixth FA Cup win, there was a New Year's Day fixture to play, and the visit of Bristol City to enjoy. City had been promoted in the same 1975/76 season that we made it back into the top flight but had not been able to match Albion's development as a force in Division One, having twice narrowly escaped relegation. 1978/79 was to see them consolidate in a mid-table position, but it's safe to say that their arrival at The Hawthorns held few fears for the Baggies. What did concern us was the wintry weather that was busily decimating the holiday programme, snow and ice threatening to prevent the game taking place. But Albion were desperate to get the game on, not least because they held something of a competitive advantage over their opponents, as Tony Brown explains.

"It was the back-end of December when that bad winter really started to come, and as far as I remember, that New Year's Day, we were about the only team in the country that managed to get a game on, and to be honest we were lucky to do that. We were the first team to wear those pimple boots and that made all the difference for us – I think Willie Johnston had recommended them to us, because he'd played on Astroturf in them. We'd used them in training and they were brilliant, especially when the snow came. They gave you great grip on what was just a sheet of ice to be perfectly honest.

57

"Bristol City's manager at the time was Alan Dicks and he wanted the game calling off because he thought it was dangerous, so him and Ron Atkinson were stood in the tunnel with the referee before the game discussing what they should do. Big Ron said it was fine because he was desperate to play, so he said, "Tell you what, some of our lads will put their boots on and they'll go and run about on it and we'll see how it goes." So we put these pimple boots on and it was a breeze, we were running about, turning, doing all sorts, no problem! So seeing us having no bother with the conditions persuaded the ref and Alan Dicks that it was all fine, and so they agreed to play.

"When the game started, they'd got their normal boots with studs on and they could barely stand up and we just ran rings round them, murdered them and finished up winning 3-1. Ally Brown got a couple and John Wile scored as well. It was marvellous how you could keep your feet in those boots, when they were just slipping and sliding all over the place – they only scored with a penalty. They had to retake it after Ally Brown threw a snowball at their player when he was taking the first one! Laurie was on fire; the pitch was made for someone with such perfect balance – he could have played on it in his normal boots! He just danced on it, gliding over the surface.

"I suppose the ref might have thought about abandoning the game, but we were virtually the only game on in the country; everybody's eyes were on us; there was a crowd of more than 30 thousand in there on a freezing cold day; all paid good money for some Bank Holiday entertainment, so I don't think he dared stop it, especially as we were finding it so easy. You can't abandon a game because it's harder for one team than the other to play!

"The run we were on, to be honest, I think we'd have turned them over any road, but I know they were fuming afterwards; they knew they'd been done! It was important for us to get games on though because, even though we'd not had many postponed by then, with the FA Cup coming up and the UEFA Cup as well, we needed to make sure we played whenever we could, because we thought we could just go on winning and winning."

Level on points with Liverpool after the same number of games at the season's midway point was a nice way to celebrate New Year's Day, especially as the FA Cup was next up, a chance to relieve the intensity of league competition, especially as Coventry City, Albion's rabbit, were the opponents. The game was postponed to the following midweek, the Baggies held to a 2-2 draw at Highfield Road on the Tuesday night before trekking off to Norwich for another massive league fixture on the Saturday.

Winter was closing in everywhere, Liverpool falling victims to it that day, so that Albion knew a point would take them to the top of the First Division. And the samba beat of Albion's attacking football just pounded on, Cyrille Regis latching onto the ball just outside the box, dragging his shot across the face of goal and into the far corner. Although the poor man's Tony Brown — World cup winner Martin Peters! — snatched an equaliser for the Canaries, Albion fans began the interminable journey home from Carrow Road with the blue and white stripes a point clear of Bob Paisley's Liverpool, an incredible achievement that had been built on ten wins and three draws in the thirteen league games, and three months since they'd last tasted defeat at the beginning of October. It was a special day for everyone connected with Albion, especially veterans like Bomber. "Norwich held no fears for us and we were disappointed we only picked up a draw. But it put us on top of the league for the first time in years, the first time I'd ever been top of the league at that stage of a season any road! It was new territory for us and a great achievement, and we deserved to be up there at the time."

John Wile echoes those thoughts, adding, "Good teams need a bit of arrogance, and that side had that edge without going over the top. We were sure of ourselves, and wherever we went, we were confident of getting a result, and we often thought a draw away from home was a bad day. The players used to demand from each other; that was the great strength; we expected each other to be at our best all the time. John Giles started that; he insisted you didn't accept anything less than 100% from yourself nor from a team-mate. That was a huge asset. No matter whether you'd fell out with anybody, with the manager, whatever, when you got on the pitch on Saturday, you would play; you wouldn't let yourself, the other players, or the crowd down. That was expected of all of us."

Not only did Albion go top of the league that day, but also their substitute underlined the scope of their ambitions at the time. Unable to get a game, David Mills sat in the dugout, just a few days after the Baggies had broken the British transfer record to get him, spending £516,000 to secure the signature of Middlesbrough's star striker. According to Wile, it was a signing that, in theory at least, had long been on the cards.

"We all thought that Ron was determined to break the transfer record, to put us on the map. But we never thought he'd do it with David Mills! We'd all played against him; he was a good player but never one you saw as outstanding in that way. We've ribbed Ron mercilessly ever since, and he always vowed afterwards that he'd never sign a player on a Sunday again because that was the day he signed David! None of the problems were down to David because he was as honest a player as you could wish for, but it turned into a disaster. When he was on his game, he was a good athlete, good clean striker of the ball, but his touch went to pieces. And never in a million years was he going to replace Tony Brown, which was the thinking behind it."

Like all true sportsmen, Bomber thrived on the competition, as Ron Atkinson ruefully concedes. "Bomber had his swansong season I suppose. He played a bit afterwards but that was his last great season. Unbelievable finisher, never bothered about anything other than sticking the ball in the net. Did his work for the team, but if there was a chance, he was onto it."

And what did Tony Brown himself make of it all? "David had a good goalscoring record at Middlesbrough. He scored goals for fun there; he got a few caps for England B I think, and he was the name you saw week in, week out on Boro's scoresheet. Every week, you picked up the paper on Sunday, and invariably you'd find that he'd scored for them again. Signing David was a big thing for Albion because we were pushing for the top and then we broke the British transfer record, which was a real show of ambition I suppose. We got all the headlines for signing the first ever £500,000 player, which was an absolute fortune in those days, it was still a few weeks before Brian Clough spent a million on buying Trevor Francis from the Blues, so for Albion to have come up with that kind of cash was unbelievable really and great publicity for us. But it all went belly up, very sour very quickly. He came in but he never really hit it off from day one; I don't know why. Maybe the price tag got to him, we'll never know.

"It's still a mystery as to why it didn't work out for him, but I'm sure that part of the problem was that when he came here, because we were playing so well, he couldn't force his way into the team and he was stuck on the bench for weeks, and probably the pressure built up on him a bit, week by week, because he couldn't get involved, and when he did get a chance to come on, people expected him to be a super-sub or something.

"David's arrival gave me a little bit of a push. I knew I was towards the end of my career, but I had a burst of goals and that kept him sitting and waiting for a chance, and that probably didn't do him any good. From day one, nothing went right for him, and it was a shame because he was a really terrific lad. He was a true professional, absolutely genuine, honest as the day is long in matches and in training; you couldn't have asked for more. He gave it everything but it just went wrong.

"In the end you have to say signing him was a mistake, and Big Ron took a lot of stick for it as well. Then the fans turned on David and that didn't help. They really got on his back after a while because they expected a lot from him because of the money involved; they expected goals, because that was what he'd been bought for – and the fee we paid was probably more than we'd paid for the rest of the team put together! The fans gave him a torrid time at the finish, and he got very down at one stage; he'd come in for training and he'd be very low, and it was understandable really, he's only human. He just got to the point where there was no way back, and you have to cut your losses and he just had to get out of the place, which I'm sure was a real relief for him."
The Mills saga was a perfect example of how delicate the balance is in any side, especially one built so much on flair and individual genius as Albion's side was. You can pay a fortune and still not get the player that takes you on to the next level.

"That's the risk you always take when you go into the transfer market; however good the player is and however much money you spend, you can never be sure whether it's going to come off, how they'll react to a new club, if they'll fit in, if they'll settle. David had been a long time at Middlesbrough. I think he'd started there as a kid, and sometimes, when you go out of that environment and things you've been used to, it just doesn't suit you. But I think probably the pressure of the fee was the hardest thing for him to deal with it was too big a weight on his shoulders."

For Mills, it was nigh on impossible to break into a side that was steamrollering its way through the First Division, and nor could he get into the FA Cup side that took on Coventry just two days later. As Bomber explains, "We thumped them 4-0 up here; I got a couple and even Brendon managed to get a goal, which was about right because it was always a doddle against them at home!"

With such a hectic schedule of fixtures and with the addition of Mills to the squad, it's surprising that changes weren't made to the team to freshen it up. That's the way it would be today, but 25 years ago, you played your best side, no matter what, as John Wile agrees.

60

"As a player you didn't want to be rested, to have squad rotation, to miss games. You wanted to play. And managers picked their first eleven and they wanted to play those players whenever they could. Nowadays, I think people want to make the game a bit more complicated than perhaps what it is; it's almost a self-preservation society in some respects, because football is no more difficult today than it was in 1978, in 1958 or 1928. It's still eleven against eleven, kicking a football. The rules haven't changed that much. Fitness levels are much higher of course, but in principle, the people who pay their money still know who can play and who can't. We had a solid eleven, we had good back up in Tucker Trewick, who would play anywhere you asked him, and we got by with those twelve really for much of the season. The team picked itself. I don't know if supporters were bored by that, thinking, "Bloody hell, not Wile and Robertson again!"

As events turned out, an enforced rest was coming. In the grip of the worst winter since 1962/63, the country was blanketed in snow. Only 12 First Division games were played in the whole of January – Albion had been lucky in getting two played. But after defeating Coventry, they would sit on the sidelines for another 19 days waiting for the weather to turn. The test they would face then was Liverpool, at Anfield.

CHAPTER TEN
EASY TO SLIP AWAY

In the deep midwinter of 1978/79, things started to go awry for the Baggies. Having gone top of the table at Carrow Road on January 13th, the side were forced to put their league duties on hold for a the rest of the month, the only football that they could shoehorn in coming in the FA Cup when they won a replay against Coventry. Nineteen game-less days passed before they could take their 19-game unbeaten run on to its sternest test, the trip to Anfield to take on Liverpool.

Daunting at the best of times, there was every reason to expect that the Reds would have something special planned for this one. Having lost the League Championship to Nottingham Forest the season before – and their European crown in a first-round defeat at Clough's hands too – there was every incentive for them to regain the title they viewed as their personal property, if only to ensure that they qualified for the Champions' Cup the following year, since you had to win it to be in it in those days.

Albion were the latest pretenders to the throne, and as such, they were a side Liverpool particularly wanted to beat, especially as that Norwich draw had elevated Albion to the top of the tree. If that wasn't bad enough, in the interim period Everton had managed to get a game played too, their 1-1 draw with Aston Villa sending them into second, level with the Baggies and a point ahead of Liverpool. If that weren't enough, while Albion had endured nearly three weeks of inactivity, Liverpool had carried on playing, in the FA Cup if not the league; the three extra games helping them maintain form and fluency.

But the way Albion had played through December and into the New Year, that all seemed to count for little, and the side travelled to Liverpool in good heart and full of confidence as Tony Brown remembers.

"We had had a fabulous run of games that stretched back about four months and when you're getting results, and especially when you're playing the way that we were, you just start to feel like you're invincible, and it doesn't matter who you're up against. If you look at that run we had, we took on Valencia, Manchester United, Arsenal, Leeds, all great sides, plus the Villa, Wolves and Birmingham in hard local derbies and had come through it all.

"It was always a massive job on whenever you went to Anfield, but we didn't fear anybody; we'd had a massive run without losing, and we felt we were going to get something out of the game and stay top of the tree. But that was an exceptional side they had that season, even by Liverpool's standards, which were as high as anything you've ever seen in this country, no question. They were brilliant, absolutely brilliant. The sad part about it was that we just didn't really perform that day. Whether it was the occasion that got to us I really don't know, but we didn't have the same rhythm and we were below par, and you can't go to Anfield and not be at your very best and hope to get a result.

"It finished up with us losing 2-1 though I think Laurie Cunningham had a good chance to equalize for us very late on in the game and missed it. That defeat was a huge disappointment to all of us because we'd been flying up until then, and if we had gone there and got something, it really would have started people thinking about us as potential champions come the end of the season. It was a massive blow to lose to them, but they were out to prove a point to us and to everybody else after we'd knocked them off the top of the table at Norwich – I can tell you that they weren't too happy about that!"

Liverpool's continuing success was in part about making good business decisions as much as good footballing decisions as Ron Atkinson explains. "As we were stuck on our backsides, Liverpool had recognized the value of undersoil heating, and they were playing all their home games without any problem, and in those days, every game at Anfield was a home win pretty much! When we kicked off against them, we did look decidedly rusty for half that game, but the longer it went on, the more we got into it and maybe we could have nicked a draw at the finish."

Defeat at Anfield was no disgrace given that most of Europe's finest had met the same fate there down the years. Bomber Brown played through the Shankly and Paisley eras and is well placed to assess just how good the 1978/79 vintage was in their pantheon of great sides. He was decidedly impressed.

"You look at the record for that season and they were pretty much unstoppable. They won 30 games out of 42, they only let in 16 goals, scored 85 goals, only lost four matches; that's a pretty awesome record no matter what era you're talking about. That broke the record for least goals conceded and for most points in a season under the old two points for a win system. To be honest, you deserve to win the league after that – you can't argue with records like that can you?! They were a genuinely world class outfit at the time; they'd won the European Cup twice in a row, which proves their pedigree. We were chasing them hard, and we thought we could match them, but they had that little bit extra, that quality, the depth in squad and the experience. And in fairness to ourselves, they also had the advantage of undersoil heating at Anfield!"

By 1978/79 Bob Paisley had been at the helm for five seasons, fine-tuning the mighty red machine that Bill Shankly had built. Were there any differences in visiting Anfield in the Paisley era compared with the legendary Shankly years?

"Not at all, because they were every bit as formidable under Bob as they had been under Shanks, and you knew you were always in for a torrid time. The thing with Bill was that he was a much more intimidating figure than Bob was. Bob was a quiet, gentle fella where Bill was always looking to be more in your face, playing psychological warfare with you. Shanks would stand in the corridor and wait for you to get off the bus and go into the away dressing room. He'd watch you off the coach, eye all of you up, just nodding away at you, and that was unheard of! Bill had this aura about him and it certainly got to teams.

"You'd see him there, and you'd start wondering what it was he'd be saying about you in their dressing room! The Liverpool lads used to tell you afterwards that he'd tell them that you looked like you'd been out in a nightclub all night, that so and so was limping, that you looked terrified! It worked; it got his players going. People think the stories about him are exaggerated, but they're not; he was an absolute legend. Bob was very different, very quiet, but he was every bit as successful in his own way, a marvellous manager, and to be able to follow Shanks, that was some task, but he did it superbly."

Liverpool dominated English football for a decade or more, much as Manchester United have done. Did Bomber ever get close to their secret?

"They had great, great players throughout the team, internationals with bags of experience. They'd built their team over fifteen or twenty years under Shankly and then Paisley, where ours had come together in a very short space of time, and it was a brilliant spell. If they needed to replace a great player, they'd get another one. When Kevin Keegan left, they brought in Kenny Dalglish, that kind of thing; all the best players wanted to go there, they had the money that other sides didn't. Alan Hansen was fabulous at the back, they had Ray Clemence in goal. Graeme Souness who, was just as influential for them as Bryan Robson was for us, he was tremendous. There's no secret; they bought the best players you could get!"

Looking back, February 1978 was perhaps the month where, had we but known it at the time, Albion's championship challenge finally came off the rails, just weeks after they had scaled the summit of the First Division. Most frustrating of all – and it's an anguish that many share to this day – was the fact that Albion fell by the wayside as a result of factors which, for the most part, were beyond their control. The biggest villain in the 1978/79 season was the weather, snow and ice gripping the country for weeks on end and leaving the Baggies desperately trying to get games on. And all the while, they were sitting around with the memory of defeat at Anfield at the forefront of their minds, a result that became more galling by the weeks as Liverpool's undersoil heating allowed then to carry on pretty much as normal on Merseyside.

And the 2-1 defeat did prey on the players' minds, as Tony Brown remembers. "That defeat knocked us back a little bit and we then had virtually the rest of February off in the league; we only played once more that month, three weeks later when we lost at home to Leeds. I think if we could have played again the week after we lost at Liverpool, we'd have got it out of our system. When you've lost one, you want to get out there again as soon as you can to put it right, but we didn't get that chance.

"We had to sit around for a long while after the Liverpool game, moping about that one for a bit, as they carried on playing and opened a bit of a gap up if I remember right. We were struggling just to find somewhere to train never mind playing. Our training was nearly all indoors; we had to find gymnasiums to work in because it was impossible to work outside. And it's not the same then; you can't do your proper work, breaks your routine up and that was a really boring time, kicking your heels really.

"You can't keep your match sharpness because it doesn't matter how hard you train, that is something else completely, and it was almost like coming out of pre-season when we played again, because you only have that real edge from playing regular games. If you have a long spell away from it, it dulls you a bit. We couldn't go abroad because they were always hoping to shoehorn games in here and there, so you had to be ready for them, and it was a nightmare time. We did a lot of work at GKN's place in Smethwick; they had a good gym there, and that was our home pretty much, along with Spring Road a bit, but the GKN place was a bit bigger. But it's no substitute for playing outside, and we lost momentum as a result."

It was three weeks before Albion played competitively, meaning the Liverpool game had been the only one of consequence over the course of 40 days, a football fast that left Albion in the wilderness as Liverpool played on, putting five points between themselves and the Baggies, having played just one game more, a decisive blow in the context of the season.

In preparation for the resumption of football, Ron Atkinson had done everything in his power to try to retain Albion's fluency, including arranging friendlies around the country. "We got a game in at Portsmouth just after the Liverpool game and then stopped again. We lost our rhythm when the bad weather came, and I specifically remember us flying out to Guernsey to play Birmingham City – the two of us chartered a planes and that must have been the only ground anywhere that you could get a game on – it was like a parks game; we played on a pitch with a rope around it to keep the crowd back! Then one night we went over to Witney to play what must have been the most competitive friendly I've ever seen against Nottingham Forest. Witney's normal crowd was about 800 people, but on that night there were five times that many, because I think it was Trevor Francis' first or second game for them after he moved there for a million! But it was no substitute for proper football, which Liverpool carried on playing. They got a few extra games played, more points on the board, and they were in pole position by the time we got up and running again."

The Leeds United game on February 24th was another must win for Albion, but this time they didn't, in spite of Tony Brown grabbing a first-half lead thanks to a trademark volley from the edge of the box. Leeds fought back to win 2-1 and leapfrog them in the table, West Brom slumping to fifth and a distant, perhaps irretrievable, seven points from Liverpool. The freeze had been particularly unkind to Albion, only Nottingham Forest having played fewer games, while the club had still to play its fourth-round FA Cup tie against, ironically, Leeds United. Having been drawn away to them, the game still took place at The Hawthorns after they'd been banned from playing FA Cup ties at Elland Road because of the thuggish behaviour of some of their fans the previous season.

Visits from Leeds at that time were always special events, hugely atmospheric, bordering on the savage, particularly at night, under lights. And that's how the two teams reconvened on the Monday night. And again on the Thursday night after the match went to a replay – police overtime pay must have gone through the roof that week. Bomber Brown remembers the on-field action though. "We had a couple of epic FA Cup games with Leeds, and we were just desperately trying to cram the games in because of the weather. The first was a cracking game, but they got two in the last ten minutes, equalized right at the death to make it 3-3, and we had to go and play another replay, which was the last thing we needed.

"The replay was at The Hawthorns 72 hours after the first one, which was hard work – there's no way you could put a replay on inside 72 hours these days; the club and the police just wouldn't stand for it. But we played on and we got to the end of the game and it was 0-0, and we had to go through extra time, which was even worse! There was no penalties in those days either; you just carried on having replays until you got a final result, and if we'd gone to another replay it'd have been on a neutral ground, which would have been great for them, and to be honest, I think that was what they played for that night; they were a lot more negative than in the first game. Thankfully we dug it out and won 2-0 in extra time.

"You pass it, I'll shoot!" Tony Brown gives John Wile some advice
(Picture: Laurie Rampling)

"Who did it Cyrille? I'll get him..." Robson's on a mission
(Picture: Laurie Rampling)

"Taxi for Laurie!" Ally Brown calls a cab
(Picture: Laurie Rampling)

On a slow boat in China: Bryan Robson wishes he was in Alicante, May 1978
(Picture: Graham Silk)

"Mr Chairman! Can you believe the shirts Coventry are wearing?" Tony Brown receives the matchball with which
he broke Albion's goalscoring record from Bert Millichip, October 21st 1978 (Picture: Laurie Rampling)

One degree under. Batson and Regis accompanied by Wayne Hughes in China
(Picture Graham Silk)

From Red Square to Red Star, Albion take the field in Belgrade, March 7th 1979
(Picture WBA Archive)

Life with the lions: Director Sid Lucas and chairman Bert Millichip in China, May 1978 (Picture: Graham Silk)

"I'll hold your cigar while you sign!" Ron Atkinson in obliging mood (Picture: WBA Archive)

"That's not Dalglish behind me is it?" Tony Godden ready for action (Picture Laurie Rampling)

PROGRAMME PARADE
SEASON 1978-9

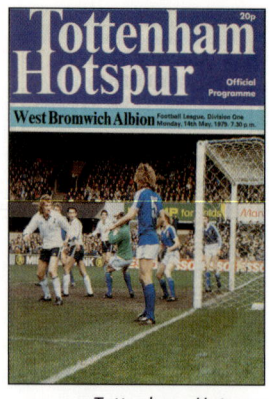

Tottenham Hotspur

Manchester United

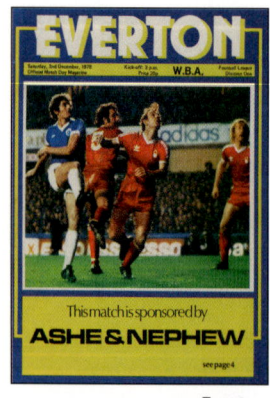

Everton

Birmingham City

Coventry City

Red Star Belgrade

Red Star Belgrade

Liverpool

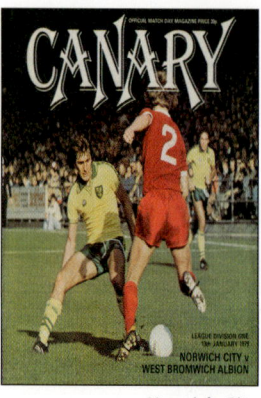

Norwich City

Coventry City

Arsenal

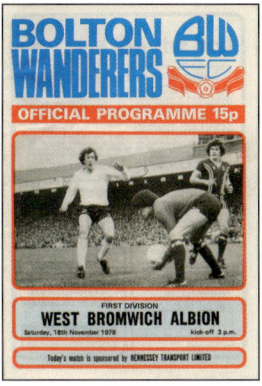

Bolton Wanderers

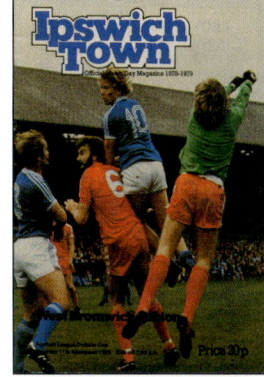

Ipswich Town

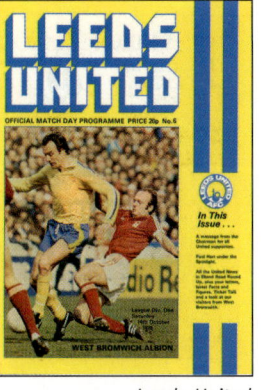

Leeds United

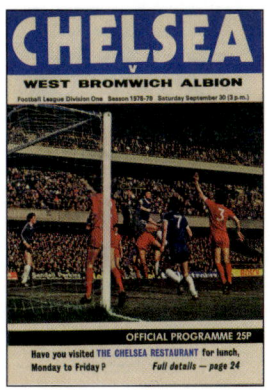

Chelsea

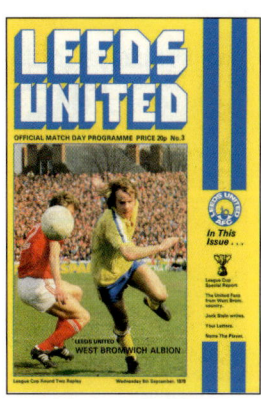

Leeds United

Nottingham Forest

Tennent Caledonian Cup

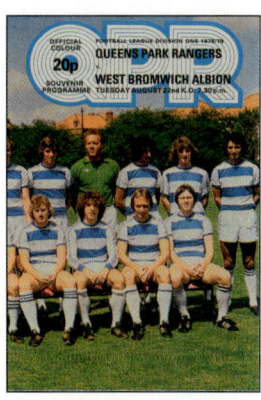

Queens Park Rangers

Middlesbrough

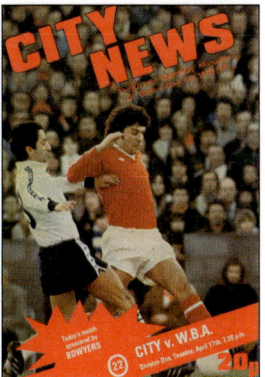

Bristol City

Aston Villa

Watched by the Woodman, Ally Brown v Ipswich Town, August 19th 1978

"John Wile scored a volley; he absolutely leathered one in, which shows how confident we were when your centre half is up there slamming volleys in! I don't care what dressing room you take me into, there was no better dressing room anywhere than ours at that moment in time. Everybody was up for it; there were so many good players, great lads as well. We came along together and just gelled straight away. I played for a long time, won a few medals and that, but there was never any side that I played in that could match that one, not even the 1968 side. For pure quality and individual skill, that team had everything you wanted."

Character was key according to captain Wile. "The dressing room was full of great lads who would do anything you asked them to do, be it visiting supporters' clubs, going to a hospital, looking after somebody; we'd all share the load and I can't speak highly enough of all of them. I know the memory gets softer as time goes on, but you wouldn't wish to meet a better set of lads. We carried that spirit onto the pitch."

That spirit was about to be tested to breaking point in a March where fixtures piled one on top of another. Make or break time.

CHAPTER ELEVEN

THE FACTS OF LIFE

A chink of light appeared for Albion's championship challenge at the beginning of March. Playing their fourth game inside a week, they took maximum points on their travels – they were playing Coventry, it was inevitable. As the Baggies were winning by three goals to one, David Mills scoring on his full debut, Liverpool were astonishingly held o-o at Stamford Bridge by a Chelsea side that was sinking fast along with Birmingham City at the foot of the First Division. Yet more astoundingly, they were held again three days later, o-o, by the same Coventry side that couldn't stop shipping goals every time Albion turned up. Funny old game.

The Baggies were now seven points adrift of Paisley's team, but with two games in hand, offering a glimmer of hope with which to head off to Belgrade for the fourth-round UEFA Cup tie, a game for which Mills was ineligible. There was also another crucial absentee for Albion, as Ron Atkinson remembers. "Len Cantello was a terrific player, and before the game against Red Star, he was taken ill, and we missed him for a few games, and that was a big blow because he was really important to the balance of the team. Him missing that game out in Belgrade might have been the difference between us getting beat and getting a o-o."

Tony Brown was a big Cantello fan too, saying, "He was exactly the same as Bryan, rock hard, wouldn't let anybody get past him, did the sitting job in the middle of the park, allowed us to play from the back by picking the ball off the central two, and he allowed Pop to get forward a lot as well by holding the midfield. Len probably didn't get a lot of the credit because there were more glamorous players in the side and the hype around it, but Len was a really superb footballer and a great winner.

"That game, his place was taken by John Trewick, who was very important for us because he'd come in and do a job for us in the midfield if we had injuries or suspensions, and he was a very under rated footballer was John. He was a good player, passed it really well; you could always rely on him to give a solid performance, but with Bryan Robson and Len Cantello doing so well, and Bryan having an injury-free season for once, it was hard for him to break into the team as a regular. That team more or less picked itself for long spells during that season assuming everybody was available, and John couldn't quite get in, which was a shame because he was a real quality midfield player. He liked possession, liked to pass it, always wanted to keep it simple so that you never gave the ball away, just kept things ticking over nicely in the middle of the park, very much in the mould of Johnny Giles.

"There's absolutely no doubt for me that playing under Johnny had a massive influence on John Trewick. People used to say Gilesy himself was one of them that John Trewick would be the natural successor to him in the middle of the park for us, and you can't get a much higher compliment than that. But while he was here, he was always a bit in the shadow of Bryan Robson maybe, and he couldn't quite fulfil that promise and go on and make the shirt his own which was a shame. And to live up to the title of being the next Johnny Giles would be hard for anybody, because that's some pressure. Gilesy was the best player I ever worked with at the Albion, no doubt. His knowledge of the game was second to none.

"After Gilesy went and Big Ron came in and he had his own ideas, and he thought about changing things a bit, but when he saw how things were going, the quality of our training the five-a-sides we had were brilliant he realised he didn't need to change anything; he'd have been stupid to do anything like that. He had brilliant players, good professionals who worked hard, looked after themselves and knew what they were about. Probably all he did was make us a bit more attack-minded, asked us to get the ball forward a bit quicker, and maybe that didn't help John Trewick's case either because he'd go for a more patient build-up, the way Gilesy had."

The Johnny Giles blueprint was, of course, ideal for European football, and it's no coincidence that Trewick had many of his best games that season in the UEFA Cup, including the trip to Belgrade. Having overcome Valencia so comprehensively, some Albion fans thought the club was odds-on to lift the trophy, but that was to dangerously underestimate one of the best sides in Europe, a team using all the advantages that professional sportsmen could enjoy behind the Iron Curtain to build a remorseless, ruthless, uncompromising outfit that was incredibly difficult to break down. Eastern European en counters were always an education in those days, and this was no exception according to Tony Brown.

"I'll never forget going out to Belgrade to play Red Star. It was unbelievable; they had this huge open bowl of a stadium, I can see it now, and it was packed with 95,300 people; the noise was deafening and it was a terrific atmosphere, very hostile, but the kind of game you want to play in. That was why you worked so hard to qualify for Europe, those amazing nights of football; as players you love to get out in those environments, and test their ability and their character in places that are totally different, totally foreign to you. Those are the occasions that you work all your life for. That's what playing at the top is about. They were special games, special nights. And where do you play in front of 90-odd thousand these days? I can't think of many places that hold that many, maybe the Maracana in Rio or somewhere, but that was a huge crowd to play in front of and something I'll always remember."

Going to Belgrade in 1979 really was a case of venturing deep into the heart of the communist bloc and very much into the unknown, especially as it was a decade since the Baggies previous competitive trip into a similar nation when they played Dinamo Bucharest in the 1968/69 Cup-Winners' Cup. Bomber remembers finding himself in a very different world once he got off the plane in Belgrade.

"Since the Berlin Wall came down and the Cold War finished and all of that, it's probably very different now, but people forget, back then, a trip to Belgrade really was going behind the Iron Curtain, right into the unknown. It was a very strange trip, very alien, a different world. They were very dour people, a different way of life; they didn't have the freedom that we took for granted and you could see that all round you, how they were treated; it was a totally different way of life. We were chaperoned everywhere; you weren't allowed to go and have a look at anything on your own, you always had to be with the official party; they were very strict with that. It was very much a Big Brother sort of thing; you felt people were always watching you, wherever you were.

"We certainly did a lot of travelling that year, China, Syria, Turkey, Portugal, Spain, Yugoslavia, but when you're a top side as we were at that point, you took it for granted a bit. But that was every player's ambition, to take those games on, and to see the world by taking on the best in the world. There's nothing like it, absolutely nothing. Saying that, people get the wrong impression, because you travel the world, but you don't get to see it – my family always reckon I've seen everything there is to see, but when I was at the Albion, I saw nothing much! You might be playing in Rome, but you don't see much of Rome, the Vatican, anything, because you're basically stuck in hotels or on a bus. And if you're not there, you're training. Once you've finished training you've got to go and rest up to recover and prepare for the game, so you don't want to go traipsing around sightseeing! People think the travel bit of it all is great, but it's nothing much; you don't see a huge amount like you would if you'd gone there on holiday. You've got a professional job to do; you go out to these places to get a result and that has to come first.

"China was a little bit different because we were there on tour if you like. It was a cultural exchange thing as well, and they did put on a lot of sightseeing trips and things for us, so we had the chance to go and see the communes and so on. We went to see Chairman Mao's Mausoleum in Tianamen Square in Beijing, and that really sticks out in my mind. There were crowds of people, lines and lines up and down, for miles and miles waiting to go in there. Because we were visitors from another country, they took us down the front of the queue, and that was something to remember. That and then going to see the Great Wall of China were the things that I really remember from that trip, but to be honest, it was very unusual to see that much when we were away really. In Belgrade, we barely saw anything. If there was anything much to see!"

The way the Yugoslavs played was typical of the more cynical side of European football first pioneered by some of the Italian and English sides of the 1960s but honed to perfection by Red Star.

69

"They were full of little tricks to try and beat you, very physical and cynical on the field. We were well-drilled before the game not to react to any of it because they were out to get you sent off for retaliation, and we were well-disciplined, but it was hard work. They were trying to provoke all of us for 90 minutes, but we just looked at concentrating totally on our football as the best way to respond. There was a lot of niggly stuff; they didn't let the game flow, but you can't just say it was an eastern European trick because there was no side as good at it as Leeds United back here, so I suppose we were ready for it!"

The Red Star game was a massive one for the club, for difficult though it was, the UEFA Cup represented perhaps Albion's best chance of glory according to John Wile. "I think the break because of the weather maybe made us feel that the league was beyond us, but I think we felt confident about the cups, certainly the UEFA Cup, having beaten Valencia. The longer we weren't playing, as confident as we were, the more we felt out of it. We knew we'd been on fire before the snow came, and that gnawed at us. There was a loss of confidence that we could win it because there were just too many games to play and too much to do. Losing at Liverpool just compounded that, and from there we were always chasing them, and they were a great side, no two ways about it. But in a straight cup tie, we felt we could beat anybody."

Albion and Red Star certainly were very keenly-matched, and for once, it was a game in which Albion's game plan rested very much on their defence, a much neglected but utterly vital component in that swashbuckling season, Cyrille Regis admitting, "We went out there determined not to concede.The boys at the back were vital for us. John Wile and Ally Robertson were rock solid, and they had a perfect understanding from years of playing together, then you had Brendon and Derek on either side who could use the ball, get forward, defend strongly, and they were the foundation because we had licence to pour forward with that insurance behind us. They were a terrific base to work from. We could be cavalier, creative, imaginative, take risks, knowing they would save us if things went wrong, and that's what all good sides have, however attack-minded they are."

As the captain and the man at the heart of the defensive system, who better than John Wile to explain how the back four was organised? "People talk about systems, formations, but we used to play basically two at the back, myself and Alistair. Brendon and Derek, in front of us, pushed onto their wingers because the two of us were comfortable with dealing with anything knocked over the top, sweeping it up. In doing that, Derek and Brendon were principally there to support the attack, and with them playing so high, we had Bomber and Bryan Robson given the chance from midfield to go and support the forwards. If you watch Manchester United now, when the ball goes in the opposition box, there are always at least four United players in there, so it's no wonder they get goals. But those players get back as well to defend when they have to. And that's what that side did well. If you do that, if your midfield support, you score goals.

"Brendon was a terrific introduction to the side down the right, but on the left we had Derek Statham, who in some ways was the best player we had in that team, ahead of Laurie, Bryan, Cyrille. Derek is the best left-back I've ever seen. If he'd played at Arsenal and Kenny Sansom had been here, Derek would have had 80 caps. Incredible player, so much ability, quick, brave. He was small, which was the only disadvantage he had compared with Sansom, not so good in the air, but he was a better tackler, better going forward, better footballer all round. He made his debut at Stoke and scored, went on a run from halfway and belted it in. That's Class!

"It's a cheap phrase but Derek was international class, no doubt about that, and had he had the chance to prove it, he could have been world class. He used to frighten you to death! He'd get it on the edge of our box, we'd be screaming at him to get rid of it, but he'd roll his foot over it, drag it back between his legs, turn, and play his way out of trouble."

Ron Atkinson insists that "Little Statham was the best fullback I ever worked with", but that's nothing compared with the praise Tony Brown lavishes on him. "I've got to admit, Derek Statham is one of my all-time favourite players at the Albion, or anywhere else for that matter. He had such tremendous ability and so many attributes, it's hard to know where to start when you're talking about him because he was one of the real greats. He had terrific confidence in his own ability, which was probably his greatest strength I think. He was cocky, not in a nasty, arrogant way, but he just knew how good he was, how talented he was, and how he could apply it. He did things that no other player could do at that time, no other fullback any road! It was a pleasure and a privilege to play alongside him, and it was great for me because I was playing on the left of the midfield so I got to see him at real close quarters and he was terrific. He was the instigator of a lot of my goals over those two or three seasons because he would go on these runs down the left flank and took defenders with him, giving me a bit of space.

"Once he got hold of that ball, it was like it was tied to his bootlaces, because he had such tight control it was mesmerizing; you could only wonder how it was that he did it. In the modern game he would be in his element, and with England's problems down the left-hand side, he'd just walk into the team, no danger – none of the current crop could hold a candle to him. He'd be an automatic selection for England, and he would be a real star, playing at the likes of United or Chelsea.

"A couple of times a bit later on, it looked like he was on his way, because we always thought Big Ron would come back and get him for Manchester United. And then he had a move sorted out for him to go to Liverpool, and he failed his medical and it all fell through. But he never let it get him down; he carried on playing as well as he ever had, and he was just superb. To be honest, the only disappointment regarding Derek was that he should have had dozens and dozens of England caps, no doubt about it, instead of the couple he got. Injuries later on didn't help him, but it was always Kenny Sansom who got the call instead, and that was a travesty. Kenny was a good player but Derek was just a different class, not only to him, but to most other left-backs I've ever seen. But a lot of Albion lads have struggled to get into the England team over the years; you think back to Jeff Astle or to Bryan Robson, Cyrille, Laurie, great players who didn't get the caps they should have got when they were at Albion.

"Derek would be perfect for today's game, as a wing-back. He was a good defender, really strong in the tackle, but when he had the chance to go forward, he was virtually a left winger at times, so fast, such great control. He was in the team at the same time as Willie Johnston and Laurie Cunningham, and going forward, he never suffered in comparisons with them two, that's how good he was. You can't pay a higher compliment than that. Some of the things he used to do, you couldn't help but be in awe of him; he was unbelievable. You'd just stand back and be amazed. Your heart was in your mouth sometimes, and in our own penalty box, he would do things like drag-backs, little one-twos with people, which terrified you at times. You're thinking, "Get rid of the thing!" But Derek was just so cool, so composed, he'd play his way out of his own box and 30 seconds later he'd be rampaging forward and creating a chance at the other end of the field. He was just a stunning footballer."

71

If Statham was the footballing live wire, then Alistair Robertson – revered by Bryan Robson as "One of the best centre halves I ever played with" – was the man who displayed the more rugged virtues of the defensive arts. He and John Wile made 1245 Albion appearances between them, formed the greatest central defensive pairing in the club's history and have deservedly passed into folklore. Wile sums up Robertson. "You would never, ever get a more consistent player than Alistair Robertson. Week in, week out, he would give you a top performance, and the only time people noticed him was once a season when he made a mistake! He was just a terrific player and it's a mystery how he never played for Scotland. He wasn't blisteringly quick but he was quick enough. And he was a hard bugger; if he tackled you, you knew about it. He was a good footballer as well, but because he was such a hard man, people thought all he could do was kick. But that's not true. Alistair could play. He had the lot, he could head it, read the game well, everything you want from a defender. The level of performance was consistently very high, over a period of seasons, not just one year, however good the opposition, home or abroad.

"Behind us, we had Tony Godden. John Osborne had been a good goalkeeper for many years and he's still my number one Albion goalie to this day, even ahead of Russell Hoult. So it was hard for Tony to come in and take over from Ossie. If John's mind was right, he'd come and take crosses on the 18-yard line, and Tony suffered after that because initially, he felt he had to do the same, and his stature didn't allow for that. He quickly accepted we had good-enough defenders to deal with those kind of balls, so he concentrated on his assets. His shot stopping, his strength in his hands was incredible, fantastic reactions, good distributor from the back, decent organizer.

"But he benefited from the fact that the back four was almost telepathic. We were good talkers all four, but we got to know each other well. We played very high up the pitch, kept a tight line, won offsides, and that was done on a look and a glance, without a word said. We'd give the nod and step up together. When the other side were chasing, the 'keeper would launch a kick and we'd step up, offside, thanks very much, and kill the game. But we never worked on it, we just knew what we were doing. We didn't get a lot of injuries at that time, and we played a lot of games together which was a great help. That season we had a nucleus of probably 13 players who formed the team, week after week. We played a lot of them carrying an injury, but my philosophy was if I miss a game, I might not get back in! We all wanted to play every game because we didn't want to give anybody the chance of taking the shirt!"

That back four gave an object lesson in keeping things tight in the white-hot atmosphere in Belgrade, keeping the Yugoslavian side at arm's-length for 84 minutes. But just when it looked like Albion would keep their unbeaten UEFA Cup record intact, they were given a cruel and brutal lesson in the realities of European club football when Red Star used what is euphemistically known as "experience" to engineer a late goalscoring opportunity, as Wile remembers.

"We learned a lot of lessons in Europe, some the hard way because we got done against Red Star; we were a bit naïve, but we were learning how to play against the best, and all those things we added to our game. We got turned over by the referee out there. We gave away free kicks around the box which is what did us. It wasn't a free kick, but we got suckered into helping them make it look like one, knowing full well the referee would favour them. And once they got it, their lad took an absolute screamer, and nothing could keep that one out."

A single defeat in Belgrade was not the end of the world, and Albion returned to England, physically shattered but with morale high, to take on Southampton in an FA Cup fifth-round tie at The Hawthorns. But the hectic games programme wasn't the only foe they had to battle, according to John Wile. "We started playing again, and then suddenly there was an outbreak of flu in the camp, and we all got struck down by that. We played through it, made changes when we had to, but when you're playing so many games, you don't get any recovery time, and although we got over the flu itself, the effects stayed with us for the rest of the season."

With that in mind, the last thing Albion needed was a replay and an energy-sapping trip down to the south coast. So, inevitably, they got a replay and an energy-sapping trip down to the south coast, after the game at The Hawthorns ended in a 1-1 draw, Ally Brown getting Albion's goal. Such was the fixture pile-up that the replay took place just 48 hours after the first game on a Monday evening – which just goes to show not everything is Sky's idea. To make matters worse, the replay went to extra time and even then Albion didn't get the right result, as Tony Brown remembers.

"We got beaten 2-1 at The Dell in the replay which was a pity, because we were desperate to go one better than the previous season and get to Wembley – I'd have loved one last game there, but it wasn't to be. To be honest, right through my career, we never had a great record at Southampton, except when we won the cup in 1968. The Dell was a tight little ground, a really hard place to go and play, so I don't suppose it wasn't that big a shock that we got beat after we couldn't beat them at home."

On the night of March 21st 1979, The Hawthorns was absolutely heaving, packed with West Brom fans all ready to witness the destruction of another great foreign side in the mould of the Valencia game. But while there was confidence among the supporters, there was an undeniable nervousness. The defeat at The Dell that took the FA Cup away from Albion had left deep scars among the populace of West Bromwich, who were longing for a return to Wembley Stadium. It had been nine long years since we'd been back to the ground that had been a second home in those great cup-fighting years, while supporters still felt cheated that we hadn't got to the final the previous season after that superb cup run, that Ipswich had somehow stolen our trophy.

More than that though, the Albion nation was starting to fret that, although we were the best team in the land, we were going to end up empty-handed, nothing to show for these supreme efforts; a galling, terrifying prospect. Though fans still clung to the dream of overhauling Liverpool, the gap stood at a massive eight points. Though Albion had three games in hand, it would take a monumental run-in to snatch the league title, a run which, had we but known it at the time, would have needed fifteen wins and a draw to finish top of the pile. In that context, the UEFA Cup might not have quite represented the Last Chance Saloon, but it was certainly the store next door.

The players remained confident though, previous round heroics keeping spirits high according to Tony Brown. "Coming away just a single goal down and knowing what we could do at home, the goals we scored here, we fancied our chances of going through, no doubt about it. We could turn most teams over at The Hawthorns, and we felt we had a great chance. Cyrille scored a belter early on, and it was 1-0 going into the last few minutes, looking like extra time, and they suddenly had a break and equalised. With the away-goals rule that meant we had to get two goals in two minutes, so we were out.

73

"They had a bit of luck with the goal as well. Ally Robertson got in to make a block challenge and the ball just ricocheted off him and their player and it fell for them. If there was anybody I would ever stake my life on to make a tackle or a last-ditch challenge, it would have been Ally because he was just so committed to everything, but they got the break, and the lad stuck it past Tony Godden. I can still see it now it was that heartbreaking. Ally just wanted to keep possession and start another attack rather than putting it in Row Z. We were just in shock; we couldn't believe it because we'd played so well. And that was the trophy we really thought we were going to win, even if it was the hardest one, but we thought we were in with a great shout. We didn't fear anybody; we thought we could beat anyone, and after beating Valencia, we had the confidence to take on any European side and win.

"But Red Star Belgrade were a massive side, I tell you. Again, the last ten years or so and the way the eastern bloc countries have changed, you've not really heard much about sides from that part of the world because their players leave the country to get better money elsewhere, so their club football has suffered. But back then, they were a real hard proposition, like a lot of teams out there; very fit, strong, powerful. They were successful in Europe, great support, everybody knew who they were, and nobody across Europe fancied playing them. In the finish, they got to the final of the UEFA Cup and got very close to beating Borussia Moenchengladbach, who'd been runners-up in the European Cup itself just two years before, which shows you the sort of standard we're talking about."

Losing to Red Star was no disgrace, but it was a devastating blow as John Wile acknowledges. "Probably we showed our naivety in the return leg by pushing on for a winner when we could have gone for extra time and won it, and by doing that, they scored a late goal and that killed the tie. We lacked a bit of nous, the sort of patience that Liverpool showed time and again in Europe. That was a huge disappointment because we did fancy our chances in that one."

Time, as the cliché goes, to concentrate on the league.

CHAPTER TWELVE

THE LONG MARCH

Albion's challenge in the cup competitions may have lain dead in the water after the contrasting travails of Southampton and Belgrade, but Spring sprung, even in the Black Country, leaving the Baggies a dozen First Division games to wrench one piece of silverware from the season, the one we prized above all others, our first League Championship since the days of Pennington, Pearson and Morris way back in 1919/20. Standing between Albion and the title were 16 games in 58 days, all amid a tangible determination not to allow a season of such rich promise to wither on the vine.

The number of postponements Albion had had to endure, through the weather and cup commitments, had a bizarre effect on the way the season's remaining fixtures would pan out. After they travelled to collect the obligatory win at Coventry on March 3rd, they weren't required to play a First Division game away from The Hawthorns again until April 13th, giving a sequence of five games on home soil. The pressure was on, but at least here was a window of opportunity for Albion to pass through. Ten points out of ten would keep them right in the running going into the home straight.

But that very advantage could easily have imposed an unbearable burden on a side that was still uncertain of just what a return to first-team action would mean for them as Tony Brown explains.

"It was very much like starting the season all over again when we began playing in March, because we'd pretty much had the February off because of the bad weather. It was like coming back into work without the benefit of a pre-season almost! But then we got stuck into the games in March again, and it just shows you how this area of the country must have had probably the worst of the weather because, when we started playing again, we were packing in home games, because it had been them that had been postponed more regularly than our trips to away grounds. We had five home games in a row in the league, and looking back at it, that was a good way to ease yourself back into it really, and we set off great. I suppose it could have been a pressure, knowing you had to win every time you went out on the field at The Hawthorns, but I honestly can't remember any of us ever feeling that way.

"We were flying again in that little period, and you've got to give the team a fair bit of credit for that because we'd had that setback against Liverpool, but we came straight back from it pretty much and pushed on and kept ourselves right in contention up at the top, which took some doing when you were head-to-head with Liverpool. But confidence was sky-high about the place, and we were happy to take on all-comers, no danger; that was the feeling from everybody.

"When you're sitting around waiting for the weather to change, you do wonder how you'll go when you start playing again, how your form will be. Obviously you're hoping that you can just pick up from where you left off and go on winning, but you can't be sure. Ok, we had a batch of home games to get us going, but you've still got to win them, and when you're playing so many in such a short space of time it's hard, but when you win five on the trot, you're doing something right! Players from other clubs used to say they didn't like coming to The Hawthorns, and when you get that, that's a real compliment. That's what you want because you've won half the battle then, and that was how it was, not just that season, but for a few seasons either side of it."

The first three games of that run were something of a grind as Albion faced three teams who were destined to finish in the bottom four of the table, all of whom were desperately scrapping for the points that would keep them afloat come the end of the season. Fortunately none of them managed to find those points at The Hawthorns as the Baggies just did enough to collect six points out of six, beating Danny Blanchflower's all-but-bankrupt Chelsea by a single Ally Brown goal as Chelsea plummeted out of the top flight, those points coming on the Saturday before Albion entertained Red Star Belgrade in that fateful second-leg tie. But in that very midweek, Liverpool turned up the heat still further, beating Wolves 2-0 at Anfield to take an eight-point lead over Albion, who had three games in hand. The Baggies had also suffered the ignominy of slipping below Everton too, though the gap there was a slightly more manageable four points with five games in hand.

QPR were next up on Saturday March 24th as the Baggies looked to exorcise the Red Star demons with a win, and it was testimony to their character that Ally Brown and Laurie Cunningham found the goals to beat the Londoners 2-1. It was all back to Albion's place again on the Monday night to use up one of those games in hand in front of 20,010, some indication that fans in the recession hit Black Country were clearly finding their pockets stretched by the prospect of so many games in such a short space of time. Derby County took an early lead but a leg-weary Albion team found enough in the locker to come back at them in the second half, the same firm of Ally Brown and Laurie Cunningham doing the damage.

76

The rare luxury of a nine-day break between games allowed the Baggies some much-needed rest on the back of 11 games in 30 days, which encompassed four FA Cup ties and two UEFA Cup ties as well as five vital First Division matches: physically and mentally exhausting fixtures. How desperately the players needed that rest was obvious when they came back to The Hawthorns to take on middling Manchester City in midweek. City were simply spanked, Albion crushing them 4-0, with a list of unusual goalscorers including Trewick, Mills and young Kevin Summerfield, now carving out a promising coaching career for himself.

City clearly didn't relish the prospect of coming to The Hawthorns, but as Bomber remembers, they weren't alone in that at the time.

"I'm sure everybody feared us at that time because we were hard to score against, and we had goals coming from all over the team at that particular time – even David Mills got a couple for us in that spell, so he didn't have quite such a bad start as people remember! We all felt he was settling in when he scored at Coventry and against Manchester City, but it wasn't to be, and he only got one more all season, which wasn't as big a return as we wanted after we'd paid all that money; the fans expected a lot more and they got on his back. But The Hawthorns really did become a bit of a fortress at that time, and every side came here half-expecting us to turn them over; players used to tell us that after the game."

Back to second place, only four points shy of Liverpool still with a game in hand, things were starting to get interesting as the Baggies headed into the final one of that sequence of home games, by far the toughest, but one they had to win to complete the nap hand. Everton were the visitors, also needing to win if they were going to have any chance of a runners-up spot. As the season built to its climax, Albion's squad was put under intense pressure, and injuries and suspensions began to take their toll, forcing the Baggies to draw on the more peripheral members of the squad along with some younger talent from the youth system. Martyn Bennett stood in for Brendon Batson at right-back to make his first-team debut against Everton, but he gave a highly accomplished performance, rich with promise for the future, as Albion ground out a 1-0 win against a physically powerful, but overwhelmingly defensive Everton unit. Ally Brown got the goal, but it was testament to the titanic competitiveness of Bryan Robson that it was created; the tireless midfielder chasing Colin Todd down to win the ball and feed the Action Man with eight minutes to go.

Great is one of those words that gets hurled around all too easily. Painful truth though it is, in the modern age, perhaps Albion have only ever produced one truly world-class player, a player who could walk into the England side, and who would truly merit inclusion in an all-time national team, certainly in the post-war era. For all the qualities of Allen and Barlow, Regis and Cunningham, Astle and Bomber, their international careers were peripheral at best, albeit that that was in part due to the vagaries of the various national selectors.

But not even the London, Manchester and Liverpool-obsessed managers could fail to notice the astonishing qualities of the man who must surely be Albion's greatest-ever player, Bryan Robson. Although, unsurprisingly, it took the local press and a petition from Albion supporters before the then England boss, Ron Greenwood, finally noticed that Robson was head and shoulders above every other midfielder in the land and was the man around whom England should build their future. Robson is certainly grateful for the promotional push that the locals gave him.

"There was a big campaign, especially in the *Evening Mail*, to get me into the England squad, and that was a big help for me, because at the time I don't think the England scouts were watching too many of the Albion games. I'm sure that did help influence Ron Greenwood to get people to come and watch me and then things went from there."

By the time Robson did get his first international recognition, Albion fans already knew that here was one of the finest footballers they'd ever been privileged to see, comfortable on the ball, unbeatable in the tackle, courageous, a great leader, good reader of the game, composed passer and great finisher. Put simply, Bryan Robson was the complete footballer. In a team with Regis, Cunningham, Statham, Batson and all the rest, Robson was routinely the choice as the Albion man of the match, week in, week out. How great a recommendation do you need?

The one thing that kept Albion going through their hectic schedule was the togetherness in the camp and the fact that, wherever you looked in that squad, they were high-quality players all over the place. Seeing those players train maintained belief that, once the Baggies started playing again, results would inevitably come. But as the games passed by in a blur, if you needed to look for one driving force in particular, all eyes would rest on Bryan Robson, as Tony Brown points out.

"In a lot of ways, Bryan is probably the greatest player Albion have ever had, certainly in the time I've been here. He was an incredible all-rounder, was Pop. He was very unusual in that he had good touch, great strength, a great reader of the game, and he could play in any position you wanted to on the pitch, and he could do a great job. He played all over the place for us. He scored goals as a centre-forward, played left-back, and of course he was magnificent in the middle of the park, though to be honest a lot of us thought his best position was centre half. We always used to have a lot of practice matches in training, and he was brilliant in those as a centre half; it was a doddle for him, he strolled through them. He was so brave, so strong, in the tackle he was just exceptional, and when he'd got hold of the ball, he had terrific vision and he could distribute it well.

"He was a winner, a real inspiration if things weren't going right for you; he'd keep everybody going and he was a terrific fella as well. And to top it off he was a natural finisher, terrific goalscorer. Every year you could guarantee he'd get near-enough double figures in goals, and when you add that to what Cyrille would get, Ally, myself, Laurie, you can see why we had such a great season in 1978/79. He really had got the lot. He was really just a young lad at that time, but he was marvellous to play alongside, and I still think that that spell here might just have been the best football of his career because he was unbelievable. I know he had massive success with England and Manchester United after he went, but I can't believe he was any better than when he played for the Albion.

"We had Cyrille Regis, Laurie Cunningham, Derek Statham, Ally Brown, myself, John Wile, Ally Robertson, all these players, but week after week, Pop was the man of the match because he was always right at the heart of every game we played, he was the driving force behind it. He had a fantastic engine, the ability and the energy to literally cover every blade of grass on the pitch every game we played. He never got tired, even in training; he'd be up front at every session and he'd just run and run and run, you couldn't stop him. He's the sort of player that any great side needs, the driving force, the way Keane has been for United after Pop finished playing or Vieira at Arsenal. Big Ron knew just how important Robson was and that's why, as soon as he went up to Old Trafford, he spent a fortune on him, to make him the most expensive player ever; that's why he became England captain, got 90 caps and would have had about 50 more if it hadn't been for injuries. Simple really. If he was about today, he'd be worth a fortune, £30million plus, without a shadow of a doubt. He'd got the lot."

If ever Albion needed reminding of the virtues of a good youth-development system, then we need only think back to those heady days and that heady team – Ally Robertson, Derek Statham, Robson, Tony Brown, John Trewick, Len Cantello and Martyn Bennett had all made it through the ranks, saving the club an absolute fortune in transfer fees. Robson was brought down to The Hawthorns from his native County Durham as a youngster, and Bomber remembers seeing him in his early days.

"I remember him as a spindly little kid, there was nothing to him, and the club were making sure that at his digs, they were feeding him big steaks and all sorts just to try and build him up to try and make sure he'd have a good-enough physique for the game. But as he got a little bit older, he started training with us every now and then sometimes we had the kids playing in our practice matches and as soon as he got involved in that, the first-team lads started looking at each other and saying, "We've got a player here!" He'd come in and try to do everything; he was confident in his ability, a bit cocky, and you could see even then that he was going to be a bit special.

"Having Pop in the side was perfect for me because he had this great drive and energy about him, and he would give you the chance to get forward because he was happy enough and unselfish enough to do the sitting job. So if I went on a run forward, I knew that he'd be slotting in behind me and that he would give me the defensive cover, and he'd be there until I got back. And for an opposition player coming through, it must have been a terrifying proposition. You've got Bryan Robson bearing down on you, then if you get past him you've got John Wile coming at you, and if you got past him, there was Ally Robertson who would kick the living daylights out of his granny if it meant getting the ball. All three of them took no prisoners, and good players as well."

Albion would need all that they could give and more as they entered the final stretch. They had 35 days and twelve games to salvage the biggest prize of all from the centenary season.

CHAPTER THIRTEEN

WHERE DID IT ALL GO WRONG?

The quirks of football history throw up the oddest things; statistics that link different sides from different eras: elevens that have no more link with one another than bearing the same club name. Record books may show that your team hasn't won at a particular ground in 50 years, or that this side or that side hasn't beaten you in the last 35 outings. There's no logic to it, but there it is, the history books tell the tale.

Following Albion, one thing you do expect is that holiday periods will rarely see the team at its best, Christmas and Easter always seemingly costly in the final analysis. The thumping wins over Arsenal, Manchester United and Bristol City had given the lie to that over the season of goodwill, but as the Baggies readied themselves for Easter, a similarly impressive return was imperative as they took on Southampton, Arsenal and Bristol City in the space of five days, the first two on successive days, Good Friday and Easter Saturday.

Liverpool, with fewer games to cram in, had no need of playing on Good Friday and instead enjoyed a more leisurely programme, playing at Molineux three days earlier, collecting a 1-0 win to further crank up the pressure. For Albion, the game plan was simple. Win, win and win again. Simple on paper, not quite so easy in reality though, as Tony Brown remembers.

"It was just such an effort to run sometimes because we had so many games in such a short space of time, we played in heavy mud, and it was like trying to run in divers' boots sometimes, it really was. People don't realise what it takes out of you when you come to the next game: you really can't raise a gallop sometimes, you can't lift your legs up, you really are just slogging through it all. Before kick off you might feel fine, but as soon as the whistle goes and you get into the game, there were just some matches where you couldn't get going at all and that did for us really.

"The big difference to now was the standard of the pitches, there's no comparison with today's. You hardly ever see a muddy pitch these days, but most were heaps then, especially that year because of all the bad weather we'd had to put up with. And that just took its toll on the legs. You don't want to make an excuse but the facts are there.

"I think that's the big difference to these days: you don't get anything like the old Baseball Ground swamp any more! Groundsmen are better equipped for the job; there's probably not as many games played on them as there were in the old days when you had all your reserves and youth team games on there, and the pitches look a treat now; they're looked after much better than they were, and that has to be a help to the players of today. You can ping the ball about no problem; you're not ploughing through a foot of mud with the ball, and in that respect, it is a different game.

"I don't think any club would have to put up with the same fixture pile-up now, even Manchester United or Arsenal, because the authorities would change things round. But we had a nightmare run of games at the start of April, when we were still definitely in the hunt if we won our games in hand. But we played four games in a week – Southampton away which was a trek, Arsenal at home, Bristol City away, Wolves at home, and then we had Birmingham as well just a few days later, and it was an incredible period to go through. It just sucked all the energy out of you, and it told, physically and mentally, to be honest.

"It gets to the legs, no doubt about it, and we were running on empty for a lot of that period; it got to be a bit like a boxer fighting from memory after a couple of rounds too many! Going to Southampton was always a really hard one for anybody, always has been, still is nowadays, a bit like Norwich I suppose; they were a really hard team to beat on their patch under Lawrie McMenemy. The Dell was a tight little ground, very noisy, very hostile, and they had a great record there. And we had a couple of local derbies coming up against Wolves and Blues as well, and they were desperate to try and stop us. The fierceness of the derby game is always there, but they both had awful seasons - Birmingham ended up getting relegated - and to get something from their seasons they felt they had to stop us doing anything, stop us going on and challenging Liverpool, so that just geed them up a little bit more for the games to make it even harder for us. A lot of people were talking about Albion so that was all the incentive they needed to try and stop us."

A Cyrille Regis goal got us a creditable draw at Southampton, and then the following day, it was Bomber who popped up to head in for another 1-1 draw against an Arsenal side that by then were preparing for the FA Cup Final, a great disappointment to the 28,623 crowd who had gathered to see us try to turn up the heat on Liverpool. It was now 32 games, 48 points for us, 33 games and 54 points for Liverpool as the dream started to ebb away.

Perhaps the final flush of hope came on one of Albion's rare days off as Liverpool went to Villa Park and took a real hammering from the Villa, 3-1. The following night, Albion went to mid-table Bristol City knowing that, if we could win, it was game on again, but as Cyrille Regis notes, "We got out there and we were dead on our feet. That was like a bridge too far if you like, and we just couldn't gather ourselves for that final push because we were exhausted. We wanted it as badly as the fans or Ron did. We put very high demands on one another, really high; we demanded that everyone be at their best because we trusted each other. We would never let somebody else's game slip. If anyone was having a bad time, it was, "Listen, you're better than that but you're not showing me. Come on, pick it up. Show me what you can do."

"But at Bristol City, we couldn't show it any more because we were out on our feet. We took an incredible number of fans with us, about 10,000 or something, but we were gone. We didn't have the reserve strength to make changes and the lads that played were shattered. We lost 1-0 and that was that. Deep down, we knew then that we weren't going to catch Liverpool after that."

John Wile agrees with that assessment, but as captain, tried to keep things going in the face of adversity, typical of the way he led the side with such distinction for so long. "It was a fantastic side to captain. I'd been captain at Peterborough and most of the junior sides I'd played in because, by nature, I was very noisy on the field. If you play centre half and you're quiet, it's like not being able to head the ball. You've got to be a talker, an organiser; it's essential. I always had something to say and in that sense I was captain material I suppose. Don Howe gave it me when we still had Tony Brown, Jeff Astle, people like that in the team; that was a real honour at a relatively young age.

"But then to lead the team out in 1978/79, you just knew you had a part to play in directing something a bit special. And we did make changes on the field if we felt things weren't going right; we'd change it ourselves. The regular one was, "Let's all play 10 yards further up the field, play on top of the opposition." It's still one of my favourite sayings today. If I see a team under pressure, I always think they can change the picture just by playing those 10 or 12 yards higher up the pitch. All the good teams do that, but your Arsenals have the pace at the back to get away with it, just as we did."

But that pace, the vigour, the enthusiasm had been sucked out of the side by the sheer physical enormity of the task, by the heavy pitches, by the weather and by the knowledge that fate had stolen from them a golden opportunity that might never come again. In the face of that, the last thing you needed was a couple of emotionally-overwhelming local derbies against teams desperate to put the skids under you. Though Albion were on a different plane to Wolves that season, they got revenge for the Molineux mauling they'd endured before Christmas, John Richards grabbing a late equaliser after Robson put Albion ahead. It was the turn of Blues to twist the knife, when only a last minute goal from Bryan Robson salvaged a point for a side that was starting to look rather sorry for itself. A draw at Ayresome Park wasn't a bad result for an Albion side that generally fared dismally at Middlesbrough, but April petered out with Albion not having won for six games, as Tony Brown recalls.

"We drew five out of six in that spell, because we could still keep it tight at the back, we were organised; we could do all those things, but we lost that bit of spark, that zip going forwards because we couldn't do things at pace the way we had been doing them. That was a great disappointment because, looking at the run of games, we expected to pick a few wins out of that lot and they never materialised, and that put Liverpool beyond reach.

"At the back end of the season like that, when you're coming at games that you have to win, it becomes a mental thing as much as anything else, and that's where the real tiredness comes into it. It all came together at once and it told on us unfortunately, and we just couldn't make it over the finishing line, especially after we'd gone out of the cup competitions because we were so close to winning them. It helps if you're winning. If you're winning every game, you can play pretty much every day because it stops you feeling tired, but when you're scrapping for draws and that, you lose that little bit of edge. And when games keep coming, you don't really have time to get over the tiredness nor to get over any little knocks and injuries; you just have to soldier on with them.

"We'd been a free-scoring side all through the season, but we just lost a bit of rhythm through tiredness as much as anything I think, and we just couldn't get it back. It's hard to explain; it was just like slogging away. We lost that scoring streak, and that was partly because of the reputation we'd made for ourselves and the determination of every team we came up against – not just in local derbies – to stop us. Teams were very defensive against us just as a way of stopping us. And they were really up for it because we were a real scalp for them to take. It was that lack of goals that killed us really. If you don't score enough goals you won't win enough games; it's an old cliché, but it's true – we're still saying it sometimes even now!"

April ended with the Baggies facing six games to play, six points adrift of Liverpool, albeit with a game in hand. Bob Paisley's sides just didn't squander that kind of lead, so all that was left was the runners-up slot, a prestigious achievement in itself given that the club had only managed that twice before, in 1924/25 and 1953/54. Things looked better on that front, for after Nottingham Forest lost at Wolves on the final day of the month, Albion and Clough's men were level on 51 points, but Albion had a game in hand, a better goal difference and would have home advantage against Forest in the final game of the season.

Maybe the realisation that the title had gone was psychologically freeing for Albion, because they suddenly found a degree of fluency again, a second wind, as they reeled off a terrific sequence of four straight wins, the first a brilliant 2-0 win at Everton, where victory was always satisfying for Cyrille Regis in particular. "Whenever we went there, a week before the game, Big Ron would get a letter from an Everton supporter, full of stuff about me, Laurie and Brendon, telling him not to bring his monkeys to Goodison. They were a very hostile crowd there, especially towards the three of us, but there was only one way to react. Score a goal, win the game, and give it the old "Asda price" – tap your back pocket to show them you were going home with the points." Cyrille didn't score that night, but he was instrumental in setting up the opener for Mills, Robson scoring the second with a 30 yarder. On the same night, Liverpool were winning 4-1 at Burnden Park...

Manchester United were up next, and though the game hardly rekindled memories of the 5-3 Christmas spectacular, Albion were much the better side, a single Cyrille Regis goal enough to separate the two teams. Southampton were then beaten at last, at the fourth time of asking that year, with another 1-0 scoreline, Ally Brown registering his 24th and final goal of his greatest season in the stripes. John Trewick got nowhere near that number – four all season – but his last strike was equally crucial, a flying header that beat Aston Villa at Villa Park, a sweet Friday night in what was turning into a very bittersweet season.

Two games left, three points clear of Forest, second place in the bag. But Albionworld never quite works like that. They fell to a grim 1-0 defeat at White Hart Lane, Ricky Villa getting the goal Argentine revenge for Kempes' defeat in December – and 24 hours later, Forest won 2-1 at Elland Road to set up a last night showdown. Friday night at The Hawthorns, Albion v Forest, the final game of the season, Albion on 59 points, Forest 58. A draw would be enough, perhaps, in hindsight, the worst kind of halfway house for as attack-minded a side as they were. With £1,000 a man riding on the game, the Baggies couldn't put it together, as Bomber Brown admits.

"That was a massive game for all the players because being runners-up was still a huge achievement for the club; you go in the record books. We desperately wanted that; it would have been something to show for the season, but I don't think we played particularly well that night, and Trevor Francis nicked a goal for them late on to win it 1-0.

"I remember being very disappointed sitting in the dressing room afterwards, but to be fair, Forest did go on and win the European Cup the week after that, so they were a pretty useful team! Cloughie had a way of playing, players he trusted, and they were always tough to play against, and we rarely did well against them at home, other than in the cup the year before when we beat them 2-0. But I remember they gave us a real hammering up here the year after, 5-1 it was. They were a class act. All Cloughie's sides were very hard to break down, whether it was Forest or when he was at Derby before that, they epitomised all the things that he was all about."

Perhaps that final defeat summed up the season in some ways, a season where we seemed destined to always fall at the final hurdle in spite of the fact that Albion above all others, Liverpool included, had illuminated it with football of imagination, passion, adventure and, at times, genius. Albion's 59 point total would have been enough to win the title in plenty of other seasons, but it was not to be this time around, leaving the players and fans to cherish glorious memories rather than trophies, as Bomber recalls.

"When the season was over, the overriding feeling was one of disappointment because we all felt we could have done better. I think people expected us to actually win a trophy, and I think we all felt that we could have got closer to Liverpool in the league in particular. The way we started it was brilliant and we were flying right the way through until February time really. It was a terrific side, a great, great side to play in. We had a fabulous set of lads there, the dressing room was second to none, we all got on well together, the team spirit was great, we had some very talented individuals who could do their bit, we had a little bit of everything you need. The way it was going up to the turn of the year, we all thought that we were in with a great chance and that we were on the verge of something very special. But then it fell away a bit, and having built up that expectation, it turned out to be a disappointment in the finish. That team deserved to win something, and that's how teams are judged when you come down to it. What did you win? But the fact that there's barely a day goes by without somebody asking me about that team and that season just underlines that, even without winning anything, it was a very special year.

85

"What made it really hard to take was what happened when the season finished, because we were hoping this would be the start of something special, that that team would get better and better. But the disappointment was compounded by the fact that Len Cantello and Laurie Cunningham both left the club, pretty much straightaway, and it all started disintegrating. That was the beginning of us going towards that period in the wilderness if you like: right through the end of the 1980s and then through the 1990s. We were getting a great side together, we knew each other well, we were improving as a unit, we had great confidence in each other, we knew that we were capable of turning teams over. But before we had the chance to build on it, to stay together for a second year and carry on progressing, it was all taken away from us. It's just the way football goes sometimes. It was out of our hands, just a case of circumstances really. Len wanted to go back up north, Laurie had virtually sold himself to Real Madrid with the way he played in Valencia for us, and you can't battle against that kind of thing.

"In its own way, Len leaving at the end of that season was as big a blow as Laurie going, because he was a massive presence in that team, and that started the disintegration of the side and of the club a few years on. It was a personal thing for Len; he wanted to get off back to Manchester because his wife was homesick really, she had been for a while, and so they went back up there when his contract was finished, and the move he got to Bolton was just ideal for him and off he went. Len didn't want to leave because he fitted in perfectly with the way we played."

John Wile is in accord with Bomber's assessment of Cantello, but has another story on his departure. "Len was very underrated, even by our own supporters. He was comfortable on his left or right, strong tackler, good engine, great attitude. Couldn't head the ball to save his life! Always played for the team, very good player and crucial to us.

"From what I've heard subsequently, Len left for the sake of about ten or twenty quid a week. Bolton offered him a deal that was a few quid more than what we were prepared to give him, and he was off. As a club, you have to reach a line where you say "No more", but I'm not sure we'd really got to that point with Len. Laurie was different; at that stage you couldn't turn down £1 million, and when Real Madrid come for you, how can you stop a player going to a place like that?"

Ultimately, those two departures were a turning point for West Bromwich Albion, the beginning of the end had we but known it, as Tony Brown acknowledges. "It's a shame we couldn't have held that side together for five or six years as you normally would at that time, because players didn't move as much then. But freedom of contract came in and we lost players as a result of it. It would have been good to see how that team evolved because we just might have done something a little bit special. The ability was there, it matched anybody. But players had ambitions that were hard to fulfil here, especially internationally.

"There's no doubting that Pop Robson should have played a lot more times for England when he was at the Albion than he did — how he never went to the European Championships in 1980 is beyond me because he would have been first choice for me every time by then. But suddenly he went off to Manchester United, and before you know it, he's first choice in the side, captain, everything. Once you get to a big club, straightaway you're in the team, youve had big money paid for you, and suddenly the England manager is under pressure to select him. But he played just as well here as he did at United, so why didn't he get in then? That's always been a problem for clubs round here, not just us but Villa and Wolves as well — if you want to play for your country, you've got a far better chance if you play for a London club or one of the big sides like Liverpool or Manchester United, no question. So there's always the threat that you're going to lose your best players and then you can't go forward as a club. Players are ambitious; they want to play internationals on a regular basis and so you can't keep hold of them. It happened to us with Laurie and with Bryan, but to be honest, they didn't play any better anywhere else than they did for us, which is sad. They deserved recognition here."

Yet initially, the signs remained good, Cantello replaced by the promising England under-21 skipper Gary Owen, and Cunningham by the current England winger Peter Barnes, both lifted from Manchester City for a combined fee of £1.2 million, which still left a profit of £150,000 in change on the four moves., though that, and £350,000 more besides, was spent on Villa's John Deehan after Cyrille Regis was ruled out for several months with a knee injury sustained in pre-season when the Chinese national side played at The Hawthorns. But high-value transfers are no guarantee of success, and new players can upset the balance of both team and dressing room, as John Wile explains.

"Ron's problem came later on, probably after that season, when he tried to bring new players into the squad, and I think he got a bit carried away with himself really. He was sensible when he came in, saw it was a good side, gave us that extra impetus, spot on. But he always wanted players to excite him, do a trick, which is great, but not at the expense of the basics. We lost Len, who was a real grafter, and Gary Owen never quite did that. He was like a dog with a bone for an hour, all over the show, but he faded late in games. Peter Barnes was very erratic. We lost the team ethic which was a disaster for us, and I don't think Ron appreciated how important that had been in rebuilding things. It was a gradual process of teamwork and that slowly started to disintegrate.

"Peter Barnes and Gary Owen were good players, no question, but they weren't part of the group. As much as they fitted in, they were Manchester City players and they always would be, and that was a problem. And they were never as consistent as the players they replaced. We'd grown up as a group with Len, Willie. Laurie came in as it was getting together, and they were part of West Brom, but the boys that Ron bought in, John Deehan, David Mills, they found it hard to replace what had gone because they weren't as good as Tony Brown or Laurie Cunningham or whoever. A lot was expected of them, maybe too much, but maybe people didn't realise how good people like Len were until they'd gone.

"By the next season, it was a very different team; we'd lost that strong core, and it wasn't the same. John Deehan came in at the start of the season, and on a lot of money, more than the rest of us. John came in at 21, 22 and he'd got a big house in Sutton, and people like myself, Ally Brown and Alistair Robertson were ten years older and lived in smaller houses on less money, and that upsets the dressing room. Nothing against John, good luck to him, but the players who built that side deserved to be earning the same kind of rewards, and it started to nag. You don't mind that as a player if somebody is coming in and they're giving you 30 goals a season, or they're an incredible midfielder. But when they come in and they're in and out of the side, they're not making a huge difference; that eats away at the spirit of the team and we started to lose it then.

"And yet financially, at that time, Albion must have been as well off as anybody. We didn't spend a fortune on the ground, we had good crowds, we had the money from Laurie, we owned a lot of property as a club, but we didn't move on as we should have from the base the 1978/79 season gave us, and through bad management, we lost our way."

Wile wasn't alone in feeling that way, and ultimately that was to cost Albion the jewel in the crown, the player the club should have been built around, Bryan Robson. "It was after that 1978/79 season that I started to wonder about the future at Albion a bit because we really should have gone on from that season to challenge as a top side, but instead we started selling our best players. Laurie left, Len left and for me, that was a time when we should have been buying more top players, not selling them, and that was disappointing. As a player, you start to wonder if you can go on and win things, and that ultimately made me want to leave the club, because you want to win things in your career.

"Looking back on it, I think the biggest loss Albion ever had was when Mr Silk died in that air crash, because he had a lot of forward-thinking ideas and a lot of ambition for the club. He had great vision, and I think he would have taken us to be the sort of club that would really challenge Liverpool and Manchester United."

Bryan's time at The Hawthorns ended early in the 1981/82 season, just a few weeks after Ron Atkinson walked out on the club to join Manchester United as their manager in succession to Dave Sexton, leaving behind what he called, "The best team I ever managed." So good was that side that he couldn't resist taking some of it with him, robbing Albion of the backbone of an impressive unit. Remi Moses headed up the M6 and was quickly followed by Bryan Robson, who left for a British record transfer fee of £1,500,000.

"When Ron left the club, it seemed to me that that was a period where they weren't sure about where things were going, and when the likes of Manchester United come in for you, it's very hard to turn that down, just as Laurie couldn't resist Real Madrid. And it wasn't just United, Liverpool were in there as well, but Ron had a big influence on me. It was a wrench to leave the club on lots of levels. I loved my time here, the club were great with me from when I was a kid. I was married, my wife had never left the Birmingham area before so that was a big decision, she had to leave her family. But when it's your career, the chance to play for United or Liverpool is something you can't turn down. They were a big draw. I thought I'd win more trophies at either one of them and in the end I had to go."

While Robson went off to further his career, others were allowed to go when their playing careers ended, when they still had plenty to give to the football club, not least Albion's greatest servant, Tony Brown.

"Ron was great to me, even though I was a bit player after 1979. He kept me involved. I went on all the trips, played occasionally, and I was guaranteed a second testimonial which he wanted me to have. But then he went to Manchester United in 1981 and Ronnie Allen came in and said he wanted me away, and I missed out on the testimonial, which was a bit of a sad way for it all to end after all the years I'd been here. And I think it was a chance missed here to create a sort of Liverpool Boot Room mentality because we could have kept people like myself, Ally Rob, John Wile, in coaching positions after we finished. That would have been the way forward."

Instead, the club spent 20 years going backwards. Out of light cometh darkness.

CHAPTER FOURTEEN

DID IT REALLY HAPPEN?

Did it really happen? Was it all a mirage, a mass hallucination? Were Albion really the most exciting team in the country, maybe in Europe? Did this parochial club in the heart of the heavily-industrialised Midlands pioneer the destruction of racial barriers in the English game?

It did happen, for one glorious season, a flame that burned bright and glorious, an energy that consumed players and supporters alike, a monumental story that made us all family for an all-too brief but all-too wonderful moment, bringing us together: a bond that endures between us to this day, whichever side of the touchline we were on.

For all concerned it was a chapter of our lives that we still look back on with fondness, and only with pleasure, for the bitterness of that savage snow has long-since ebbed away, thawing to reveal a real pride in all the achievements of that time, as John Wile agrees. "It was something special that we were part of, and for me, it will always be a great source of pride to think that I captained that team. That really was a joy because, to be fair, any one of them could have done the job. I never took it for granted and even now, when I look back, it's something I cherish.

"Bert Millichip always used to have a party in the summer, before the season started. He'd invite all the office staff, the press, the players and their partners, and they were always great days, everybody loved it. I left at the end of the 1983 season and Bert asked me along to the do that summer, which I was very pleased about, but I'd only been there 5 minutes and the players took me to one side to say, "What are we going to do about this then?" Like I was still captain! They presented me with a silver salver and that meant a lot to me. They were a great bunch, we were very close. That was a very special time in all our lives."

Tony Brown, player of more Albion games than anyone else, is certainly not one to disagree with Wile's summary. "I can't emphasise enough just how much of an honour it was to play in that side. It really was a bit special to have a part in that. It was so enjoyable. It was incredible to go out every Saturday knowing it would be a great game. Supporters tell me that they couldn't wait for the matches to come around, which tells its own story. But people have to accept that a side that good doesn't come around very often, and if you're expecting to see football of that quality, week in, week out, you're going to be disappointed. You need so many different things to come together all at the one time, on top of which you need a bit of luck: that all the personalities and all the talents just gel as well. However hard you work and however hard you try, it's not an exact science and you do need a bit of good fortune.

"You talk to Albion supporters who remember those days, and they cherish those days because they were great times for the club. I still go to lots of supporters' club meetings and you can guarantee that, whenever I go, there'll be questions and conversation about that particular season; fans are always harking back to it. I suppose the fact that we had all that success that season, the fact that we had so many great players and great games, those were the memories that sustained people through all those grim years since then really. That was what kept people coming to the Albion and kept the attendances so high, comparatively anyway, the dream that those days might come back. It's nice to have been a part of that."

As the years go by, the legends grow bigger but that is to diminish the truth. The legacy should be flesh and blood, not overblown legend: a tale of glorious ambition faltering in the face of the great foe, nature itself.

Those players were the heart. Lose that and you take everything else with it. Albion did and they paid a heavy price: nearly 20 years of miserable underachievement when only one thing kept the club afloat, kept people turning up to games, kept the football club alive. Flickering blue-and-white visions of a golden year, of Regis and Wile, Bomber and Batson, Cunningham and Robson. They were the best of times.

CHAPTER FIFTEEN

1978-79 LEAGUE RESULTS

AS AT 23 AUGUST 1978

	P	W	D	L	F	A	GD	PTS
ASTON VILLA	2	2	0	0	5	1	4	4
LIVERPOOL	2	2	0	0	5	1	4	4
EVERTON	2	2	0	0	3	1	2	4
MANCHESTER UNITED	2	2	0	0	4	2	2	4
WBA	2	2	0	0	3	1	2	4
NORWICH	2	1	1	0	4	2	2	3
BRISTOL CITY	2	1	1	0	3	2	1	3
COVENTRY	2	1	1	0	2	1	1	3
MIDDLESBROUGH	2	1	0	1	4	3	1	2
CHELSEA	2	1	0	1	1	1	0	2
ARSENAL	2	0	2	0	3	3	0	2
MANCHESTER CITY	2	0	2	0	2	2	0	2
NOTTINGHAM FOREST	2	0	2	0	1	1	0	2
LEEDS	2	0	1	1	4	5	-1	1
BOLTON	2	0	1	1	3	4	-1	1
DERBY	2	0	1	1	2	3	-1	1
SOUTHAMPTON	2	0	1	1	3	5	-2	1
TOTTENHAM	2	0	1	1	2	5	-3	1
WOLVES	2	0	0	2	0	2	-2	0
QPR	2	0	0	2	1	3	-2	0
BIRMINGHAM	2	0	0	2	1	4	-3	0
IPSWICH	2	0	0	2	1	5	-4	0

91

SATURDAY 19TH AUGUST 1978:

Arsenal	2	Leeds	2
Aston Villa	1	Wolves	0
Bolton	1	Bristol City	2
Chelsea	0	Everton	1
Derby County	1	Manchester City	1
Liverpool	2	QPR	1
Manchester United	1	Birmingham	0
Middlesbrough	1	Coventry	2
Norwich	3	Southampton	1
Nottingham Forest	1	Tottenham	1
WBA	2	Ipswich	1

TUESDAY 22ND AUGUST 1978:

Birmingham	1	Middlesbrough	3
Bristol City	1	Norwich	1
Coventry	0	Nottingham Forest	0
Everton	2	Derby	1
Ipswich	0	Liverpool	3
Manchester City	1	Arsenal	1
QPR	0	WBA	1
Southampton	2	Bolton	2
Wolves	0	Chelsea	1

WEDNESDAY 23RD AUGUST 1978:

Leeds	2	Manchester United	3
Tottenham	1	Aston Villa	2

SATURDAY 26TH AUGUST 1978:

Birmingham 1 — Derby 1
Bristol City 1 — Aston Villa 0
Coventry 4 — Norwich 1
Everton 1 — Arsenal 0
Ipswich 3 — Manchester United 0
Leeds 3 — Wolves 0
Manchester City 1 — Liverpool 4
QPR 0 — Nottingham Forest 0
Southampton 2 — Middlesbrough 1
Tottenham 2 — Chelsea 2
WBA 4 — Bolton 0

AS AT 26 AUGUST 1978

	P	W	D	L	F	A	GD	PTS
LIVERPOOL	3	3	0	0	9	2	7	6
WBA	3	3	0	0	7	1	6	6
EVERTON	3	3	0	0	4	1	3	6
COVENTRY	3	2	1	0	6	2	4	5
BRISTOL CITY	3	2	1	0	4	2	2	5
ASTON VILLA	3	2	0	1	5	2	3	4
MANCHESTER UNITED	3	2	0	1	4	5	-1	4
LEEDS	3	1	1	1	7	5	2	3
CHELSEA	3	1	1	1	3	3	0	3
NOTTINGHAM FOREST	3	0	3	0	1	1	0	3
NORWICH	3	1	1	1	5	6	-1	3
SOUTHAMPTON	3	1	1	1	5	6	-1	3
MIDDLESBROUGH	3	1	0	2	5	5	0	2
IPSWICH	3	1	0	2	4	5	-1	2
ARSENAL	3	0	2	1	3	4	-1	2
DERBY	3	0	2	1	3	4	-1	2
MANCHESTER CITY	3	0	2	1	3	6	-3	2
TOTTENHAM	3	0	2	1	4	7	-3	2
QPR	3	0	1	2	1	3	-2	1
BIRMINGHAM	3	0	1	2	2	5	-3	1
BOLTON	3	0	0	2	3	8	-5	1
WOLVES	3	0	0	3	0	5	-5	0

SATURDAY 2ND SEPTEMBER 1978:

Arsenal	5	QPR	1
Aston Villa	1	Southampton	1
Bolton	2	Birmingham	2
Chelsea	0	Leeds	3
Derby	0	Coventry	2
Liverpool	7	Tottenham	0
Manchester United	1	Everton	1
Middlesbrough	0	Ipswich	0
Norwich	1	Manchester City	1
Nottingham Forest	0	WBA	0
Wolves	2	Bristol City	0

AS AT 2 SEPTEMBER 1978

	P	W	D	L	F	A	GD	PTS
LIVERPOOL	4	4	0	0	16	2	14	8
WBA	4	3	1	0	7	1	6	7
COVENTRY	4	3	1	0	8	2	6	7
EVERTON	4	3	1	0	5	2	3	7
LEEDS	4	2	1	1	10	5	5	5
ASTON VILLA	4	2	1	1	6	3	3	5
BRISTOL CITY	4	2	1	1	4	4	0	5
MANCHESTER UNITED	4	2	1	1	5	6	-1	5
ARSENAL	4	1	2	1	8	5	3	4
NOTTINGHAM FOREST	4	0	4	0	1	1	0	4
NORWICH	4	1	2	1	6	7	-1	4
SOUTHAMPTON	4	1	2	1	6	7	-1	4
MIDDLESBROUGH	4	1	1	2	5	5	0	3
IPSWICH	4	1	1	2	4	5	-1	3
CHELSEA	4	1	1	2	3	6	-3	3
MANCHESTER CITY	4	0	3	1	4	7	-3	3
WOLVES	4	1	0	3	2	5	-3	2
DERBY	4	0	2	2	3	6	-3	2
BIRMINGHAM	4	0	2	2	4	7	-3	2
BOLTON	4	0	2	2	5	10	-5	2
TOTTENHAM	4	0	2	2	4	14	-10	2
QPR	4	0	1	3	2	8	-6	1

AS AT 9 SEPTEMBER 1978

	P	W	D	L	F	A	GD	PTS
LIVERPOOL	5	5	0	0	19	2	17	10
COVENTRY	5	4	1	0	11	4	7	9
EVERTON	5	4	1	0	7	2	5	9
WBA	5	3	2	0	9	3	6	8
ASTON VILLA	5	3	1	1	8	3	5	7
NOTTINGHAM FOREST	5	1	4	0	3	2	1	6
SOUTHAMPTON	5	2	2	1	9	9	0	6
MANCHESTER UNITED	5	2	2	1	6	7	-1	6
LEEDS	5	2	1	2	10	8	2	5
MANCHESTER CITY	5	1	3	1	7	7	0	5
BRISTOL CITY	5	2	1	2	4	5	-1	5
NORWICH	5	1	3	1	8	9	-1	5
ARSENAL	5	1	2	2	9	7	2	4
BOLTON	5	1	2	2	7	11	-4	4
TOTTENHAM	5	1	2	2	5	14	-9	4
MIDDLESBROUGH	5	1	1	3	5	7	-2	3
IPSWICH	5	1	1	3	4	7	-3	3
CHELSEA	5	1	1	3	5	9	-4	3
WOLVES	5	1	0	4	4	8	-4	2
DERBY	5	0	2	3	4	8	-4	2
BIRMINGHAM	5	0	2	3	4	10	-6	2
QPR	5	0	2	3	3	9	-6	2

SATURDAY 9TH SEPTEMBER 1978:

Birmingham	0	Liverpool	3
Bolton	2	Derby	1
Coventry	3	Chelsea	2
Everton	2	Middlesbrough	0
Ipswich	0	Aston Villa	2
Manchester City	3	Leeds	0
Nottingham Forest	2	Arsenal	1
QPR	1	Manchester United	1
Southampton	3	Wolves	2
Tottenham	1	Bristol City	0
WBA	2	Norwich	2

SATURDAY 16TH SEPTEMBER 1978:

Arsenal 1	Bolton 0
Aston Villa 1	Everton 1
Bristol City 3	Southampton 1
Chelsea 1	Manchester City 4
Derby 3	WBA 2
Leeds 1	Tottenham 2
Liverpool 1	Coventry 0
Manchester United 1	Nottingham Forest 1
Middlesbrough 0	QPR 2
Norwich 4	Birmingham 0
Wolves 1	Ipswich 3

AS AT 16 SEPTEMBER 1978

	P	W	D	L	F	A	GD	PTS
LIVERPOOL	6	6	0	0	20	2	18	12
EVERTON	6	4	2	0	8	3	5	10
COVENTRY	6	4	1	1	11	5	6	9
WBA	6	3	2	1	11	6	5	8
ASTON VILLA	6	3	2	1	9	4	5	8
MANCHESTER CITY	6	2	3	1	11	8	3	7
NORWICH	6	2	3	1	12	9	3	7
BRISTOL CITY	6	3	1	2	7	6	1	7
NOTTINGHAM FOREST	6	1	5	0	4	3	1	7
MANCHESTER UNITED	6	2	3	1	7	8	-1	7
ARSENAL	6	2	2	2	10	7	3	6
SOUTHAMPTON	6	2	2	2	10	12	-2	6
TOTTENHAM	6	2	2	2	7	15	-8	6
LEEDS	6	2	1	3	11	10	1	5
IPSWICH	6	2	1	3	7	8	-1	5
DERBY	6	1	2	3	7	10	-3	4
QPR	6	1	2	3	5	9	-4	4
BOLTON	6	1	2	3	7	12	-5	4
MIDDLESBROUGH	6	1	1	4	5	9	-4	3
CHELSEA	6	1	1	4	6	13	-7	3
WOLVES	6	1	0	5	5	11	-6	2
BIRMINGHAM	6	0	2	4	4	14	-10	2

AS AT 23 SEPTEMBER 1978

	P	W	D	L	F	A	GD	PTS
LIVERPOOL	7	6	1	0	21	3	18	13
EVERTON	7	5	2	0	10	3	7	12
COVENTRY	7	4	2	1	11	5	6	10
WBA	7	3	3	1	12	7	5	9
MANCHESTER CITY	7	3	3	1	13	8	5	9
BRISTOL CITY	7	4	1	2	8	6	2	9
ASTON VILLA	7	3	2	2	9	5	4	8
NOTTINGHAM FOREST	7	1	6	0	6	5	1	8
MANCHESTER UNITED	7	2	4	1	8	9	-1	8
ARSENAL	7	2	3	2	11	8	3	7
NORWICH	7	2	3	2	14	12	2	7
LEEDS	7	2	2	3	11	10	1	6
DERBY	7	2	2	3	9	11	-2	6
SOUTHAMPTON	7	2	2	3	11	14	-3	6
QPR	7	2	2	3	6	9	-3	6
BOLTON	7	2	2	3	10	14	-4	6
TOTTENHAM	7	2	2	3	7	17	-10	6
IPSWICH	7	2	1	4	7	9	-2	5
MIDDLESBROUGH	7	1	2	4	7	11	-4	4
CHELSEA	7	1	2	4	7	14	-7	4
BIRMINGHAM	7	0	3	4	5	15	-10	3
WOLVES	7	1	0	6	5	13	-8	2

SATURDAY 23RD SEPTEMBER 1978:

Arsenal 1	Manchester United 1
Birmingham 1	Chelsea 1
Bolton 3	Norwich 2
Coventry 0	Leeds 0
Derby 2	Southampton 1
Everton 2	Wolves 0
Ipswich 0	Bristol City 1
Manchester City 2	Tottenham 0
Nottingham Forest 2	Middlesbrough 2
QPR 1	Aston Villa 0
WBA 1	Liverpool 1

In the slot. Bryan Robson fires in a free kick against Manchester City
(Picture: Laurie Rampling)

Thanks for the memories. Len Cantello bows out at
The Hawthorns, May 1979 (Picture: Laurie Rampling)

Mr. Albion on home turf
(Picture: Laurie Rampling)

Laurie Cunningham in full flight
(Picture: Laurie Rampling)

And it's goodnight from him. The two Ronnies, Atkinson and Greenwood.
(Picture: WBA Archive)

The magnificent seventh – Derek Statham finishes the Coventry rout (Picture: Laurie Rampling)

So much younger then. John Trewick and Bryan Robson celebrate success at the Augsburg Youth Tournament, 1974 (Picture: WBA Archive)

Even better than the real thing. Brendon Batson relaxes with a Pepsi (Picture: WBA Archive)

Action Man takes a breather. Ally Brown at Highfield Road
(Picture: Laurie Rampling)

Brendon Batson on the ball
(Picture: WBA Archive)

"Mine!" Robson beats Regis to the ball against Manchester United
(Picture: Laurie Rampling)

Guard of honour. The Baggies greet the Bomber, 21 October 1978
(Picture: Laurie Rampling)

The answer is blowing in the wind. Atkinson in training.
(Picture: WBA Archive)

The Guv'nor, Bryan Robson
(Picture: WBA archive)

SATURDAY 30TH SEPTEMBER 1978:

Aston Villa 1	Nottingham Forest 2
Bristol City 2	Everton 2
Chelsea 1	WBA 3
Leeds 3	Birmingham 0
Liverpool 3	Bolton 0
Manchester United 1	Manchester City 0
Middlesbrough 2	Arsenal 3
Norwich 3	Derby 0
Southampton 1	Ipswich 2
Tottenham 1	Coventry 1
Wolves 1	QPR 0

AS AT 30 SEPTEMBER 1978

	P	W	D	L	F	A	GD	PTS
LIVERPOOL	8	7	1	0	24	3	21	15
EVERTON	8	5	3	0	12	5	7	13
WBA	8	4	3	1	15	8	7	11
COVENTRY	8	4	3	1	12	6	6	11
BRISTOL CITY	8	4	2	2	10	8	2	10
NOTTINGHAM FOREST	8	2	6	0	8	6	2	10
MANCHESTER UNITED	8	3	4	1	9	9	0	10
NORWICH	8	3	3	2	17	12	5	9
MANCHESTER CITY	8	3	3	2	13	9	4	9
ARSENAL	8	3	3	2	14	10	4	9
LEEDS	8	3	2	3	10	6	4	8
ASTON VILLA	8	3	2	3	10	7	3	8
IPSWICH	8	3	1	4	9	10	-1	7
TOTTENHAM	8	2	3	3	8	18	-10	7
SOUTHAMPTON	8	2	2	4	12	16	-4	6
QPR	8	2	2	4	6	10	-4	6
DERBY	8	2	2	4	9	14	-5	6
BOLTON	8	2	2	4	10	17	-7	6
MIDDLESBROUGH	8	1	2	5	9	14	-5	4
WOLVES	8	2	0	6	6	13	-7	4
CHELSEA	8	1	2	5	8	17	-9	4
BIRMINGHAM	8	0	3	5	5	18	-13	3

97

SATURDAY 7TH OCTOBER 1978:

Arsenal 1	Aston Villa 1
Birmingham 1	Manchester City 2
Bolton 3	Leeds 1
Coventry 2	Ipswich 2
Derby 1	Chelsea 0
Everton 0	Southampton 0
Manchester United 3	Middlesbrough 2
Norwich 1	Liverpool 4
Nottingham Forest 3	Wolves 1
QPR 1	Bristol City 0
WBA 0	Tottenham 1

AS AT 7 OCTOBER 1978

	P	W	D	L	F	A	GD	PTS
LIVERPOOL	9	8	1	0	28	4	24	17
EVERTON	9	5	4	0	12	5	7	14
COVENTRY	9	4	4	1	14	8	6	12
NOTTINGHAM FOREST	9	3	6	0	11	7	4	12
MANCHESTER UNITED	9	4	4	1	12	11	1	12
WBA	9	4	3	2	15	9	6	11
MANCHESTER CITY	9	4	3	2	15	10	5	11
ARSENAL	9	3	4	2	15	11	4	10
BRISTOL CITY	9	4	2	3	10	9	1	10
ASTON VILLA	9	3	3	3	11	8	3	9
NORWICH	9	3	3	3	18	16	2	9
TOTTENHAM	9	3	3	3	9	18	-9	9
LEEDS	9	3	2	4	15	13	2	8
IPSWICH	9	3	2	4	11	12	-1	8
QPR	9	3	2	4	7	10	-3	8
DERBY	9	3	2	4	10	14	-4	8
BOLTON	9	3	2	4	13	18	-5	8
SOUTHAMPTON	9	2	3	4	12	16	-4	7
MIDDLESBROUGH	9	1	2	6	11	17	-6	4
WOLVES	9	2	0	7	7	16	-9	4
CHELSEA	9	1	2	6	8	18	-10	4
BIRMINGHAM	9	0	3	6	6	20	-14	3

AS AT 14 OCTOBER 1978

	P	W	D	L	F	A	GD	PTS
LIVERPOOL	10	9	1	0	33	4	29	19
EVERTON	10	6	4	0	13	5	8	16
NOTTINGHAM FOREST	10	4	6	0	14	8	6	14
WBA	10	5	3	2	18	10	8	13
MANCHESTER CITY	10	5	3	2	17	10	7	13
MANCHESTER UNITED	10	4	5	1	14	13	1	13
COVENTRY	10	4	4	2	14	10	4	12
TOTTENHAM	10	4	3	3	10	18	-8	11
ARSENAL	10	3	4	3	15	12	3	10
ASTON VILLA	10	3	4	3	13	10	3	10
BRISTOL CITY	10	4	2	4	11	12	-1	10
NORWICH	10	3	3	4	18	18	0	9
QPR	10	3	3	4	8	11	-3	9
LEEDS	10	3	2	5	16	16	0	8
IPSWICH	10	3	2	5	11	13	-2	8
SOUTHAMPTON	10	2	4	4	13	17	-4	8
BOLTON	10	3	2	5	16	22	-6	8
DERBY	10	3	2	5	10	19	-9	8
MIDDLESBROUGH	10	2	2	6	13	17	-4	6
WOLVES	10	3	0	7	8	16	-8	6
CHELSEA	10	2	2	6	12	21	-9	6
BIRMINGHAM	10	0	3	7	6	21	-15	3

99

SATURDAY 14TH OCTOBER 1978:

Aston Villa 2	Manchester United 2
Bristol City 1	Nottingham Forest 3
Chelsea 4	Bolton 3
Ipswich 0	Everton 1
Leeds 1	WBA 3
Liverpool 5	Derby 0
Manchester City 2	Coventry 0
Middlesbrough 2	Norwich 0
Southampton 1	QPR 1
Tottenham 1	Birmingham 0
Wolves 1	Arsenal 0

SATURDAY 21ST OCTOBER 1978:

Arsenal 1	Southampton 0
Birmingham 0	Aston Villa 1
Bolton 2	Manchester City 2
Derby 2	Tottenham 2
Liverpool 2	Chelsea 0
Manchester United 1	Bristol City 3
Middlesbrough 2	Wolves 0
Norwich 2	Leeds 2
Nottingham Forest 1	Ipswich 0
QPR 1	Everton 1
WBA 7	Coventry 1

AS AT 21 OCTOBER 1978

	P	W	D	L	F	A	GD	PTS
LIVERPOOL	11	10	1	0	35	4	31	21
EVERTON	11	6	5	0	14	6	8	17
NOTTINGHAM FOREST	11	5	6	0	15	8	7	16
WBA	11	6	3	2	25	11	14	15
MANCHESTER CITY	11	5	4	2	19	12	7	14
MANCHESTER UNITED	11	4	5	2	15	16	-1	13
ARSENAL	11	4	4	3	16	12	4	12
ASTON VILLA	11	4	4	3	14	10	4	12
BRISTOL CITY	11	5	2	4	14	13	1	12
COVENTRY	11	4	4	3	15	17	-2	12
TOTTENHAM	11	4	4	3	12	20	-8	12
NORWICH	11	3	4	4	20	20	0	10
QPR	11	3	4	4	9	12	-3	10
LEEDS	11	3	3	5	18	18	0	9
BOLTON	11	3	3	5	18	24	-6	9
DERBY	11	3	3	5	12	21	-9	9
MIDDLESBROUGH	11	3	2	6	15	17	-2	8
IPSWICH	11	3	2	6	11	14	-3	8
SOUTHAMPTON	11	2	4	5	13	18	-5	8
WOLVES	11	3	0	8	8	18	-10	6
CHELSEA	11	2	2	7	12	23	-11	6
BIRMINGHAM	11	0	3	8	6	22	-16	3

FRIDAY 27TH OCTOBER 1978:

Aston Villa 0   Middlesbrough 2

SATURDAY 28TH OCTOBER 1978:

Bristol City 1   Arsenal 3
Chelsea 3   Norwich 3
Coventry 2   Birmingham :
Everton 1   Liverpool 0
Ipswich 2   QPR 1
Leeds 4   Derby 0
Manchester City 2   WBA 2
Southampton 0   Nottingham Forest 0
Tottenham 2   Bolton 0
Wolves 2   Manchester United 4

AS AT 28 OCTOBER 1978

	P	W	D	L	F	A	GD	PTS
LIVERPOOL	12	10	1	1	35	5	30	21
EVERTON	12	7	5	0	15	6	9	19
NOTTINGHAM FOREST	12	5	7	0	15	8	7	17
WBA	12	6	4	2	27	13	14	16
MANCHESTER CITY	12	5	5	2	21	14	7	15
MANCHESTER UNITED	12	5	5	2	19	18	1	15
ARSENAL	12	5	4	3	19	13	6	14
COVENTRY	12	5	4	3	17	18	-1	14
TOTTENHAM	12	5	4	3	14	20	-6	14
ASTON VILLA	12	4	4	4	14	12	2	12
BRISTOL CITY	12	5	2	5	15	16	-1	12
LEEDS	12	4	3	5	22	18	4	11
NORWICH	12	3	5	4	23	23	0	11
MIDDLESBROUGH	12	4	2	6	17	17	0	10
IPSWICH	12	4	2	6	13	15	-2	10
QPR	12	3	4	5	10	14	-4	10
SOUTHAMPTON	12	2	5	5	13	18	-5	9
BOLTON	12	3	3	6	18	26	-8	9
DERBY	12	3	3	6	12	25	-13	9
CHELSEA	12	2	3	7	15	26	-11	7
WOLVES	12	3	0	9	10	22	-12	6
BIRMINGHAM	12	0	3	9	7	24	-17	3

SATURDAY 4TH NOVEMBER 1978:

Arsenal 4	Ipswich 1	
Aston Villa 1	Manchester City 1	
Bolton 0	Coventry 0	
Derby 4	Wolves 1	
Liverpool 1	Leeds 1	
Manchester United 1	Southampton 1	
Middlesbrough 0	Bristol City 0	
Norwich 2	Tottenham 2	
Nottingham Forest 0	Everton 0	
QPR 0	Chelsea 0	
WBA 1	Birmingham 0	

AS AT 4 NOVEMBER 1978

	P	W	D	L	F	A	GD	PTS
LIVERPOOL	13	10	2	1	36	6	30	22
EVERTON	13	7	6	0	15	6	9	20
WBA	13	7	4	2	28	13	15	18
NOTTINGHAM FOREST	13	5	8	0	15	8	7	18
ARSENAL	13	6	4	3	23	14	9	16
MANCHESTER CITY	13	5	6	2	22	15	7	16
MANCHESTER UNITED	13	5	6	2	20	19	1	16
COVENTRY	13	5	5	3	17	18	-1	15
TOTTENHAM	13	5	5	3	16	22	-6	15
ASTON VILLA	13	4	5	4	15	13	2	13
BRISTOL CITY	13	5	3	5	15	16	-1	13
LEEDS	13	4	4	5	23	19	4	12
NORWICH	13	3	6	4	25	25	0	12
MIDDLESBROUGH	13	4	3	6	17	17	0	11
QPR	13	3	5	5	10	14	-4	11
DERBY	13	4	3	6	16	26	-10	11
IPSWICH	13	4	2	7	14	19	-5	10
SOUTHAMPTON	13	2	6	5	14	19	-5	10
BOLTON	13	3	4	6	18	26	-8	10
CHELSEA	13	3	4	7	15	26	-11	8
WOLVES	13	3	0	10	11	26	-15	6
BIRMINGHAM	13	0	3	10	7	25	-18	3

SATURDAY 11TH NOVEMBER 1978:

Birmingham 5	Manchester United 1
Bristol City 4	Bolton 1
Coventry 2	Middlesbrough 1
Everton 3	Chelsea 2
Ipswich 0	WBA 1
Leeds 0	Arsenal 1
Manchester City 1	Derby 2
QPR 1	Liverpool 3
Southampton 2	Norwich 2
Tottenham 1	Nottingham Forest 3
Wolves 0	Aston Villa 4

AS AT 11 NOVEMBER 1978

	P	W	D	L	F	A	GD	PTS
LIVERPOOL	14	11	2	1	39	7	32	24
EVERTON	14	8	6	0	18	8	10	22
WBA	14	8	4	2	29	13	16	20
NOTTINGHAM FOREST	14	6	8	0	18	9	9	20
ARSENAL	14	7	4	3	24	14	10	18
COVENTRY	14	6	5	3	19	19	0	17
MANCHESTER CITY	14	5	6	3	23	17	6	16
MANCHESTER UNITED	14	5	6	3	21	24	-3	16
ASTON VILLA	14	5	5	4	19	13	6	15
BRISTOL CITY	14	6	3	5	19	17	2	15
TOTTENHAM	14	5	5	4	17	25	-8	13
NORWICH	14	3	7	4	27	27	0	13
DERBY	14	5	3	6	18	27	-9	13
LEEDS	14	4	4	6	23	20	3	12
MIDDLESBROUGH	14	4	3	7	18	19	-1	11
SOUTHAMPTON	14	2	7	5	16	21	-5	11
QPR	14	3	5	6	11	17	-6	11
IPSWICH	14	4	2	8	14	20	-6	10
BOLTON	14	3	4	7	19	30	-11	10
CHELSEA	14	2	4	8	17	29	-12	8
WOLVES	14	3	0	11	11	30	-19	6
BIRMINGHAM	14	1	3	10	12	26	-14	5

AS AT 18 NOVEMBER 1978

	P	W	D	L	F	A	GD	PTS
LIVERPOOL	15	12	2	1	40	7	33	26
EVERTON	15	8	7	0	20	10	10	23
WBA	15	9	4	2	30	13	17	22
NOTTINGHAM FOREST	15	6	9	0	18	9	9	21
ARSENAL	15	7	5	3	26	16	10	19
MANCHESTER UNITED	15	6	6	3	23	24	-1	18
ASTON VILLA	15	6	5	4	21	13	8	17
COVENTRY	15	6	5	4	19	20	-1	17
TOTTENHAM	15	6	5	4	20	26	-6	17
MANCHESTER CITY	15	5	6	4	23	18	5	16
NORWICH	15	4	7	4	28	27	1	15
BRISTOL CITY	15	6	3	6	19	19	0	15
DERBY	15	6	3	6	20	28	-8	15
LEEDS	15	4	5	6	24	21	3	13
MIDDLESBROUGH	15	5	3	7	20	19	1	13
QPR	15	3	6	6	11	17	-6	12
SOUTHAMPTON	15	2	7	6	16	23	-7	11
IPSWICH	15	4	2	9	14	22	-8	10
BOLTON	15	3	4	8	19	31	-12	10
CHELSEA	15	2	4	9	18	32	-14	8
WOLVES	15	3	1	11	12	31	-19	7
BIRMINGHAM	15	1	3	11	13	28	-15	5

SATURDAY 18TH NOVEMBER 1978:

Arsenal 2	Everton 2
Aston Villa 2	Bristol City 0
Bolton 0	WBA 1
Chelsea 1	Tottenham 3
Derby 2	Birmingham 1
Liverpool 1	Manchester City 0
Manchester United 2	Ipswich 0
Middlesbrough 2	Southampton 0
Norwich 1	Coventry 0
Nottingham Forest 0	QPR 0
Wolves 1	Leeds 1

AS AT 22 NOVEMBER 1978

	P	W	D	L	F	A	GD	PTS
LIVERPOOL	16	12	3	1	40	7	33	27
EVERTON	16	9	7	0	23	10	13	25
WBA	15	9	4	2	30	13	17	22
NOTTINGHAM FOREST	15	6	9	0	18	9	9	21
ARSENAL	15	7	5	3	26	16	10	19
COVENTRY	16	7	5	4	23	22	1	19
MANCHESTER UNITED	16	6	6	4	23	27	-4	18
TOTTENHAM	16	6	6	4	20	26	-6	18
ASTON VILLA	16	6	5	5	21	15	6	17
MANCHESTER CITY	15	5	6	4	23	18	5	16
LEEDS	16	5	5	6	26	22	4	15
NORWICH	15	4	7	4	28	27	1	15
BRISTOL CITY	16	6	3	7	19	20	-1	15
DERBY	16	6	3	7	22	32	-10	15
MIDDLESBROUGH	16	5	3	8	21	21	0	13
SOUTHAMPTON	16	3	7	6	18	23	-5	13
QPR	15	3	6	6	11	17	-6	12
IPSWICH	16	5	2	9	16	23	-7	12
BOLTON	16	3	4	9	19	34	-15	10
WOLVES	16	4	1	11	13	31	-18	9
CHELSEA	16	2	4	10	19	34	-15	8
BIRMINGHAM	16	2	3	11	16	28	-12	7

TUESDAY 21ST NOVEMBER 1978:

Birmingham	3	Bolton	0
Bristol City	0	Wolves	1
Coventry	4	Derby	2
Everton	3	Manchester United	0
Ipswich	2	Middlesbrough	1
Southampton	2	Aston Villa	0

WEDNESDAY 22ND NOVEMBER 1978:

Leeds	2	Chelsea	1
Tottenham	0	Liverpool	0

105

SATURDAY 25TH NOVEMBER 1978:

Birmingham 1	Bristol City 1
Bolton 0	Nottingham Forest 1
Chelsea 0	Manchester United 1
Coventry 1	Arsenal 1
Derby 2	QPR 1
Leeds 4	Southampton 0
Liverpool 2	Middlesbrough 0
Manchester City 1	Ipswich 2
Norwich 0	Everton 1
Tottenham 1	Wolves 0
WBA 1	Aston Villa 1

AS AT 25 NOVEMBER 1978

	P	W	D	L	F	A	GD	PTS
LIVERPOOL	17	13	3	1	42	7	35	29
EVERTON	17	10	7	0	24	10	14	27
WBA	16	9	5	2	31	14	17	23
NOTTINGHAM FOREST	16	7	9	0	19	9	10	23
ARSENAL	16	7	6	3	27	17	10	20
COVENTRY	17	7	6	4	24	23	1	20
MANCHESTER UNITED	17	7	6	4	24	27	-3	20
TOTTENHAM	17	7	6	4	21	26	-5	20
ASTON VILLA	17	6	6	5	22	16	6	18
LEEDS	17	6	5	6	30	22	8	17
DERBY	17	7	3	7	24	33	-9	17
MANCHESTER CITY	16	5	6	5	24	20	4	16
BRISTOL CITY	17	6	4	7	20	21	-1	16
NORWICH	16	4	7	5	28	28	0	15
IPSWICH	17	6	2	9	18	24	-6	14
MIDDLESBROUGH	17	5	3	9	21	23	-2	13
SOUTHAMPTON	17	3	7	7	18	27	-9	13
QPR	16	3	6	7	12	19	-7	12
BOLTON	17	3	4	10	19	35	-16	10
WOLVES	17	4	1	12	13	32	-19	9
BIRMINGHAM	17	2	4	11	17	29	-12	8
CHELSEA	17	2	4	11	19	35	-16	8

SATURDAY 2ND DECEMBER 1978:

Arsenal 1		Liverpool 0
Bristol City 1		Derby 0
Ipswich 2		Leeds 3
QPR 1		Bolton 3
Southampton 1		Birmingham 0

AS AT 2 DECEMBER 1978

	P	W	D	L	F	A	GD	PTS
LIVERPOOL	18	13	3	2	42	8	34	29
EVERTON	17	10	7	0	24	10	14	27
WBA	16	9	5	2	31	14	17	23
NOTTINGHAM FOREST	16	7	9	0	19	9	10	23
ARSENAL	17	8	6	3	28	17	11	22
COVENTRY	17	7	6	4	24	23	1	20
MANCHESTER UNITED	17	7	6	4	24	27	-3	20
TOTTENHAM	17	7	6	4	21	26	-5	20
LEEDS	18	7	5	6	33	24	9	19
ASTON VILLA	17	6	6	5	22	16	6	18
BRISTOL CITY	18	7	4	7	21	21	0	18
DERBY	18	7	3	8	24	34	-10	17
MANCHESTER CITY	16	5	6	5	24	20	4	16
NORWICH	16	4	7	5	28	28	0	15
SOUTHAMPTON	18	4	7	7	19	27	-8	15
IPSWICH	18	6	2	10	20	27	-7	14
MIDDLESBROUGH	17	5	3	9	21	23	-2	13
QPR	17	3	6	8	13	22	-9	12
BOLTON	18	4	4	10	22	36	-14	12
WOLVES	17	4	1	12	13	32	-19	9
BIRMINGHAM	18	2	4	12	17	30	-13	8
CHELSEA	17	2	4	11	19	35	-16	8

SATURDAY 9TH DECEMBER 1978:

Birmingham 1	Everton 3
Bolton 3	Wolves 1
Chelsea 0	Aston Villa 1
Coventry 1	QPR 0
Derby 1	Manchester United 3
Leeds 1	Bristol City 1
Liverpool 2	Nottingham Forest 0
Manchester City 1	Southampton 2
Norwich 0	Arsenal 0
Tottenham 1	Ipswich 0
WBA 2	Middlesbrough 0

AS AT 9 DECEMBER 1978

	P	W	D	L	F	A	GD	PTS
LIVERPOOL	19	14	3	2	44	8	36	31
EVERTON	18	11	7	0	27	11	16	29
WBA	17	10	5	2	33	14	19	25
ARSENAL	18	8	7	3	28	17	11	23
NOTTINGHAM FOREST	17	7	9	1	19	11	8	23
COVENTRY	18	8	6	4	25	23	2	22
MANCHESTER UNITED	18	8	6	4	27	28	-1	22
TOTTENHAM	18	8	6	4	22	26	-4	22
LEEDS	19	7	6	6	34	25	9	20
ASTON VILLA	18	7	6	5	23	16	7	20
BRISTOL CITY	19	7	5	7	22	22	0	19
SOUTHAMPTON	19	5	7	7	21	28	-7	17
DERBY	19	7	3	9	25	37	-12	17
MANCHESTER CITY	17	5	6	6	25	22	3	16
NORWICH	17	4	8	5	28	28	0	16
IPSWICH	19	6	2	11	20	28	-8	14
BOLTON	19	5	4	10	25	37	-12	14
MIDDLESBROUGH	18	5	3	10	21	25	-4	13
QPR	18	3	6	9	13	23	-10	12
WOLVES	18	4	1	13	14	35	-21	9
BIRMINGHAM	19	2	4	13	18	33	-15	8
CHELSEA	18	2	4	12	19	36	-17	8

AS AT 16 DECEMBER 1978

	P	W	D	L	F	A	GD	PTS
LIVERPOOL	20	14	3	3	44	9	35	31
EVERTON	19	11	8	0	28	12	16	30
WBA	18	11	5	2	36	14	22	27
ARSENAL	19	9	7	3	30	17	13	25
NOTTINGHAM FOREST	18	8	9	1	20	11	9	25
MANCHESTER UNITED	19	9	6	4	29	28	1	24
COVENTRY	19	8	6	5	25	27	-2	22
TOTTENHAM	19	8	6	5	22	28	-6	22
LEEDS	20	7	7	6	35	26	9	21
ASTON VILLA	19	7	7	5	24	17	7	21
BRISTOL CITY	20	8	5	7	23	22	1	21
SOUTHAMPTON	20	6	7	7	25	28	-3	19
NORWICH	18	4	9	5	29	29	0	17
DERBY	20	7	3	10	25	39	-14	17
MANCHESTER CITY	18	5	6	7	26	24	2	16
IPSWICH	20	7	2	11	23	28	-5	16
MIDDLESBROUGH	19	6	3	10	28	27	1	15
QPR	19	4	6	9	15	24	-9	14
BOLTON	20	5	4	11	25	40	-15	14
WOLVES	19	4	1	14	14	38	-24	9
BIRMINGHAM	20	2	4	14	18	34	-16	8
CHELSEA	19	2	4	13	21	43	-22	8

109

SATURDAY 16TH DECEMBER 1978:

Arsenal 2	Derby 0	
Aston Villa 1	Norwich 1	
Bristol City 1	Liverpool 0	
Everton 1	Leeds 1	
Ipswich 3	Bolton 0	
Manchester United 2	Tottenham 0	
Middlesbrough 7	Chelsea 2	
Nottingham Forest 1	Birmingham 0	
QPR 2	Manchester City 1	
Southampton 4	Coventry 0	
Wolves 0	WBA 3	

FRIDAY 22ND DECEMBER 1978:

Bolton 3 — Manchester United 0

SATURDAY 23RD DECEMBER 1978:

Chelsea 0 — Bristol City 0
Coventry 3 — Everton 2
Derby 0 — Aston Villa 0
Leeds 3 — Middlesbrough 1
Manchester City 0 — Nottingham Forest 0
Tottenham 0 — Arsenal 5

AS AT 23 DECEMBER 1978

	P	W	D	L	F	A	GD	PTS
LIVERPOOL	20	14	3	3	44	9	35	31
EVERTON	20	11	8	1	30	15	15	30
WBA	18	11	5	2	36	14	22	27
ARSENAL	20	10	7	3	35	17	18	27
NOTTINGHAM FOREST	19	8	10	1	20	11	9	26
COVENTRY	20	9	6	5	28	29	-1	24
MANCHESTER UNITED	20	9	6	5	29	31	-2	24
LEEDS	21	8	7	6	38	27	11	23
ASTON VILLA	20	7	8	5	24	17	7	22
BRISTOL CITY	21	8	6	7	23	22	1	22
TOTTENHAM	20	8	6	6	22	33	-11	22
SOUTHAMPTON	20	6	7	7	25	28	-3	19
DERBY	21	7	4	10	25	39	-14	18
MANCHESTER CITY	19	5	7	7	26	24	2	17
NORWICH	18	4	9	5	29	29	0	17
IPSWICH	20	7	2	11	23	28	-5	16
BOLTON	21	6	4	11	28	40	-12	16
MIDDLESBROUGH	20	6	3	11	29	30	-1	15
QPR	19	4	6	9	15	24	-9	14
CHELSEA	20	2	5	13	21	43	-22	9
WOLVES	19	4	1	14	14	38	-24	9
BIRMINGHAM	20	2	4	14	18	34	-16	8

AS AT 26 DECEMBER 1978

	P	W	D	L	F	A	GD	PTS
LIVERPOOL	21	15	3	3	47	9	38	33
EVERTON	21	12	8	1	31	15	16	32
WBA	19	12	5	2	38	15	23	29
ARSENAL	21	10	7	4	36	19	17	27
NOTTINGHAM FOREST	20	8	11	1	21	12	9	27
LEEDS	22	8	8	6	40	29	11	24
BRISTOL CITY	22	9	6	7	28	22	6	24
MANCHESTER UNITED	21	9	6	6	29	34	-5	24
COVENTRY	21	9	6	6	28	34	-6	24
ASTON VILLA	21	7	9	5	26	19	7	23
TOTTENHAM	21	8	7	6	24	35	-11	23
SOUTHAMPTON	21	6	8	7	25	28	-3	20
DERBY	22	7	5	10	26	40	-14	19
NORWICH	19	4	10	5	30	30	0	18
MANCHESTER CITY	20	5	7	8	26	25	1	17
IPSWICH	21	7	3	11	24	29	-5	17
BOLTON	22	6	5	11	29	41	-12	17
MIDDLESBROUGH	21	6	4	11	30	31	-1	16
QPR	20	4	7	9	17	26	-9	15
WOLVES	20	5	1	14	16	39	-23	11
CHELSEA	21	2	6	13	21	43	-22	10
BIRMINGHAM	21	2	4	15	19	36	-17	8

111

TUESDAY 26TH DECEMBER 1978:

Arsenal 1	WBA 2
Aston Villa 2	Leeds 2
Bristol City 5	Coventry 0
Everton 1	Manchester City 0
Ipswich 1	Norwich 1
Manchester United 0	Liverpool 3
Middlesbrough 1	Bolton 1
Nottingham Forest 1	Derby 1
QPR 2	Tottenham 2
Southampton 0	Chelsea 0
Wolves 2	Birmingham 1

SATURDAY 30TH DECEMBER 1978:

Arsenal 3	Birmingham 1	
Bristol City 1	Manchester City 1	
Everton 1	Tottenham 1	
Ipswich 5	Chelsea 1	
Manchester United 3	WBA 5	
QPR 1	Leeds 4	
Wolves 1	Coventry 1	

AS AT 30 DECEMBER 1978

	P	W	D	L	F	A	GD	PTS
LIVERPOOL	21	15	3	3	47	9	38	33
EVERTON	22	12	9	1	32	16	16	33
WBA	20	13	5	2	43	18	25	31
ARSENAL	22	11	7	4	39	20	19	29
NOTTINGHAM FOREST	20	8	11	1	21	12	9	27
LEEDS	23	9	8	6	44	30	14	26
BRISTOL CITY	23	9	7	7	29	23	6	25
COVENTRY	22	9	7	6	29	35	-6	25
MANCHESTER UNITED	22	9	6	7	32	39	-7	24
TOTTENHAM	22	8	8	6	25	36	-11	24
ASTON VILLA	21	7	9	5	26	19	7	23
SOUTHAMPTON	21	6	8	7	25	28	-3	20
IPSWICH	22	8	3	11	29	30	-1	19
DERBY	22	7	5	10	26	40	-14	19
MANCHESTER CITY	21	5	8	8	27	26	1	18
NORWICH	19	4	10	5	30	30	0	18
BOLTON	22	6	5	11	29	41	-12	17
MIDDLESBROUGH	21	6	4	11	30	31	-1	16
QPR	21	4	7	10	18	30	-12	15
WOLVES	21	5	2	14	17	40	-23	12
CHELSEA	22	2	6	14	22	48	-26	10
BIRMINGHAM	22	2	4	16	20	39	-19	8

Derek Statham mesmerises Manchester City
(Picture: Laurie Rampling)

A centenary season demands a celebratory....
Lemonade??? (Picture: WBA Archive)

David Mills settles into life on the bench
(Picture: WBA Archive)

Get 'em young: Derek Statham and John Trewick on a recruitment drive
(Picture: WBA Archive)

"Once you've seen one hotel reception, you've seen 'em all." China May 1978
(Picture: Graham Silk)

"What a lot of junk." "No, they're the big ships." Derek Monaghan, Alistair Robertson and Ally Brown
take the waters, China May 1978 (Picture: Graham Silk)

Cantello charges, Coventry capitulate
(Picture: Laurie Rampling)

He wouldn't leave footprints in snow. An afternoon at the ballet with Laurie Cunningham
(Picture: Laurie Rampling)

Terry Butcher, very tricky player. Robbo gets acquainted with a future England colleague
(Picture: Laurie Rampling)

ALBION NEWS 1978-79

Leeds United 29 Aug 1978

Norwich City 9 Sept 1978

Liverpool 23 Sept 1978

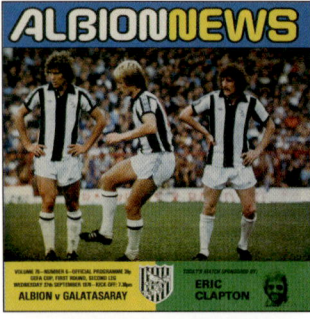

Galatasaray 27 Sept 1978

Coventry City 21 Oct 1978

Birmingham City 4 Nov 1978

Aston Villa 25 Nov 1978

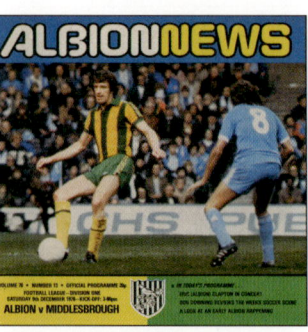

Middlesbrough 9 Dec 1978

Southampton 22 Dec 1978

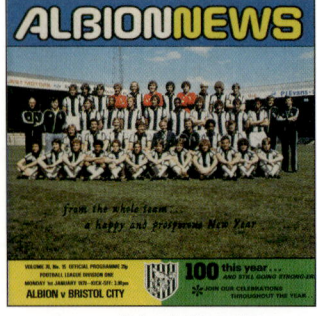

Bristol City 1 Jan 1979

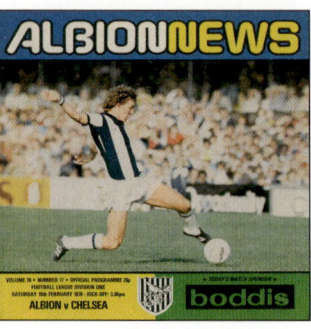

Chelsea 10 Feb 1979

Leeds United 24th Feb 1979

Southampton 10 March 1979

Red Star Belgrade 21 March 1979

QPR 24 March 1979

Derby County 26 March 1979

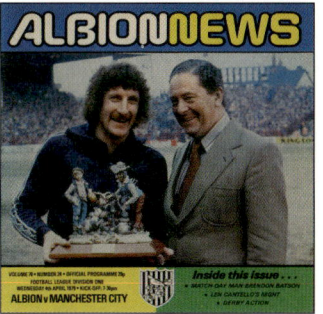

Manchester City 4 April 1979

Everton 7 April 1979

Arsenal 14 April 1979

Manchester United 5 May 1979

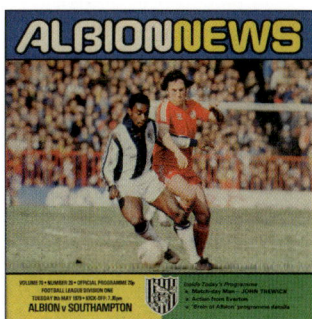

Southampton May 8 1979

*Coventry City FA Cup
3rd round replay*

Leeds United FA Cup 4th round

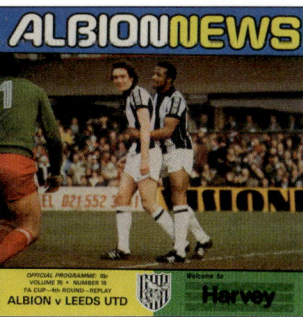

*Leeds United FA Cup
4th round replay*

Regis denied. It didn't happen often
(Picture: Laurie Rampling)

AS AT 13 JANUARY 1979

	P	W	D	L	F	A	GD	PTS
WBA	22	14	6	2	47	20	27	34
LIVERPOOL	21	15	3	3	47	9	38	33
EVERTON	22	12	9	1	32	16	16	33
ARSENAL	23	12	7	4	41	21	20	31
LEEDS	24	9	9	6	45	31	14	27
NOTTINGHAM FOREST	21	8	11	2	22	14	8	27
BRISTOL CITY	25	9	8	8	30	26	4	26
COVENTRY	22	9	7	6	29	35	-6	25
TOTTENHAM	23	8	9	6	25	36	-11	25
MANCHESTER UNITED	22	9	6	7	32	39	-7	24
ASTON VILLA	21	7	9	5	26	19	7	23
SOUTHAMPTON	21	6	8	7	25	28	-3	20
MANCHESTER CITY	22	5	9	8	28	27	1	19
NORWICH	20	4	11	5	31	31	0	19
IPSWICH	22	8	3	11	29	30	-1	19
DERBY	22	7	5	10	26	40	-14	19
BOLTON	22	6	5	11	29	41	-12	17
MIDDLESBROUGH	21	6	4	11	30	31	-1	16
QPR	21	4	7	10	18	30	-12	15
WOLVES	21	5	2	14	17	40	-23	12
CHELSEA	22	2	6	14	22	48	-26	12
BIRMINGHAM	22	2	4	16	20	39	-19	8

113

MONDAY 1ST JANUARY 1979:

WBA 3   Bristol City 1

SATURDAY 13TH JANUARY 1979:

Arsenal 2   Nottingham Forest 1

Bristol City 0   Tottenham 0

Leeds 1   Manchester City 1

Norwich 1   WBA 1

WEDNESDAY 17TH JANUARY 1979:

Wolves 2	Southampton 0

SATURDAY 20TH JANUARY 1979:

Ipswich 3	Wolves 1
Manchester City 2	Chelsea 3
QPR 1	Middlesbrough 1
Tottenham 1	Leeds 2

AS AT 20 JANUARY 1979

	P	W	D	L	F	A	GD	PTS
WBA	22	14	6	2	47	20	27	34
LIVERPOOL	21	15	3	3	47	9	38	33
EVERTON	22	12	9	1	32	16	16	33
ARSENAL	23	12	7	4	41	21	20	31
LEEDS	25	10	9	6	47	32	15	29
NOTTINGHAM FOREST	21	8	11	2	22	14	8	27
BRISTOL CITY	25	9	8	8	30	26	4	26
COVENTRY	22	9	7	6	29	35	-6	25
TOTTENHAM	24	8	9	7	26	38	-12	25
MANCHESTER UNITED	22	9	6	7	32	39	-7	24
ASTON VILLA	21	7	9	5	26	19	7	23
IPSWICH	23	9	3	11	32	31	1	21
SOUTHAMPTON	22	6	8	8	25	30	-5	20
MANCHESTER CITY	23	5	9	9	30	30	0	19
NORWICH	20	4	11	5	31	31	0	19
DERBY	22	7	5	10	26	40	-14	19
MIDDLESBROUGH	22	6	5	11	31	32	-1	17
BOLTON	22	6	5	11	29	41	-12	17
QPR	22	4	8	10	19	31	-12	16
WOLVES	23	6	2	15	20	43	-23	14
CHELSEA	23	3	6	14	25	50	-25	12
BIRMINGHAM	22	2	4	16	20	39	-19	8

WEDNESDAY 31ST JANUARY 1979:

Everton	1	Aston Villa	1
Norwich	1	QPR	1

SATURDAY 3RD FEBRUARY 1979:

Bristol City	3	Ipswich	1
Chelsea	2	Birmingham	
Leeds	1	Coventry	0
Liverpool	2	WBA	1
Manchester United	0	Arsenal	2
Middlesbrough	1	Nottingham Forest	3
Norwich	0	Bolton	0
Southampton	1	Derby	2
Tottenham	0	Manchester City	3
Wolves	1	Everton	0

AS AT 3 FEBRUARY 1979

	P	W	D	L	F	A	GD	PTS
LIVERPOOL	22	16	3	3	49	10	39	35
WBA	23	14	6	3	48	22	26	34
EVERTON	24	12	10	2	33	18	15	34
ARSENAL	24	13	7	4	43	21	22	33
LEEDS	26	11	9	6	48	32	16	31
NOTTINGHAM FOREST	22	9	11	2	25	15	10	29
BRISTOL CITY	26	10	8	8	33	27	6	28
COVENTRY	23	9	7	7	29	36	-7	25
TOTTENHAM	25	8	9	8	26	41	-15	25
ASTON VILLA	22	7	10	5	27	20	7	24
MANCHESTER UNITED	23	9	6	8	32	41	-9	24
MANCHESTER CITY	24	6	9	9	33	30	3	21
NORWICH	22	4	13	5	32	32	0	21
IPSWICH	24	9	3	12	33	34	-1	21
DERBY	23	8	5	10	28	41	-13	21
SOUTHAMPTON	23	6	8	9	26	32	-6	20
BOLTON	23	6	6	11	29	41	-12	18
MIDDLESBROUGH	23	6	5	12	32	35	-3	17
QPR	23	4	9	10	20	32	-12	17
WOLVES	24	7	2	15	21	43	-22	16
CHELSEA	24	4	6	14	27	51	-24	14
BIRMINGHAM	23	2	4	17	21	41	-20	8

SATURDAY 10TH FEBRUARY 1979:

Arsenal 0	Middlesbrough 0
Birmingham 0	Leeds 1
Coventry 1	Tottenham 3
Derby 1	Norwich 1
Everton 4	Bristol City 1
Ipswich 0	Southampton 0
Manchester City 0	Manchester United 3
QPR 3	Wolves 3

AS AT 10 FEBRUARY 1979

	P	W	D	L	F	A	GD	PTS
EVERTON	25	13	10	2	37	19	18	36
LIVERPOOL	22	16	3	3	49	10	39	35
WBA	23	14	6	3	48	22	26	34
ARSENAL	25	13	8	4	43	21	22	34
LEEDS	27	12	9	6	49	32	17	33
NOTTINGHAM FOREST	22	9	11	2	25	15	10	29
BRISTOL CITY	27	10	8	9	34	31	3	28
TOTTENHAM	26	9	9	8	29	42	-13	27
MANCHESTER UNITED	24	10	6	8	35	41	-6	26
COVENTRY	24	9	7	8	30	39	-9	25
ASTON VILLA	22	7	10	5	27	20	7	24
NORWICH	23	4	14	5	33	33	0	22
IPSWICH	25	9	4	12	33	34	-1	22
DERBY	24	8	6	10	29	42	-13	22
MANCHESTER CITY	25	6	9	10	33	33	0	21
SOUTHAMPTON	24	6	9	9	26	32	-6	21
MIDDLESBROUGH	24	6	6	12	32	35	-3	18
BOLTON	23	6	6	11	29	41	-12	18
QPR	24	4	10	10	23	35	-12	18
WOLVES	25	7	3	15	24	46	-22	17
CHELSEA	24	4	6	14	27	51	-24	14
BIRMINGHAM	24	2	4	18	21	42	-21	8

AS AT 21 FEBRUARY 1979

	P	W	D	L	F	A	GD	PTS
LIVERPOOL	24	18	3	3	56	10	46	39
ARSENAL	26	14	8	4	45	22	23	36
EVERTON	26	13	10	3	37	22	15	36
WBA	23	14	6	3	48	22	26	34
LEEDS	27	12	9	6	49	32	17	33
NOTTINGHAM FOREST	22	9	11	2	25	15	10	29
BRISTOL CITY	28	10	8	10	34	33	1	28
COVENTRY	25	10	7	8	33	40	-7	27
TOTTENHAM	26	9	9	8	29	42	-13	27
MANCHESTER UNITED	24	10	6	8	35	41	-6	26
SOUTHAMPTON	26	8	9	9	31	32	-1	25
ASTON VILLA	22	7	10	5	27	20	7	24
IPSWICH	25	9	4	12	33	34	-1	22
NORWICH	24	4	14	6	33	39	-6	22
DERBY	24	8	6	10	29	42	-13	22
MANCHESTER CITY	25	6	9	10	33	33	0	21
MIDDLESBROUGH	24	6	6	12	32	35	-3	18
BOLTON	23	6	6	11	29	41	-12	18
QPR	25	4	10	11	24	37	-13	18
WOLVES	25	7	3	15	24	46	-22	17
CHELSEA	25	4	6	15	28	54	-26	14
BIRMINGHAM	25	2	4	19	21	43	-22	8

117

TUESDAY 13TH FEBRUARY 1979:

Liverpool 1   Birmingham 0

QPR 1   Arsenal 2

SATURDAY 17TH FEBRUARY 1979:

Southampton 3   Everton 0

TUESDAY 20TH FEBRUARY 1979:

Southampton 2   Bristol City 0

WEDNESDAY 21ST FEBRUARY 1979:

Chelsea 1   Coventry 3

Liverpool 6   Norwich 0

SATURDAY 24TH FEBRUARY 1979:

Arsenal 0	Wolves 1
Birmingham 1	Tottenham 0
Bolton 2	Chelsea 1
Coventry 0	Manchester City 3
Derby 0	Liverpool 2
Everton 0	Ipswich 1
Manchester United 1	Aston Villa 1
Norwich 1	Middlesbrough 0
Nottingham Forest 2	Bristol City 0
QPR 0	Southampton 1
WBA 1	Leeds 2

AS AT 24 FEBRUARY 1979

	P	W	D	L	F	A	GD	PTS
LIVERPOOL	25	19	3	3	58	10	48	41
ARSENAL	27	14	8	5	45	23	22	36
EVERTON	27	13	10	4	37	23	14	36
LEEDS	28	13	9	6	51	33	18	35
WBA	24	14	6	4	49	24	25	34
NOTTINGHAM FOREST	23	10	11	2	27	15	12	31
BRISTOL CITY	29	10	8	11	34	35	-1	28
SOUTHAMPTON	27	9	9	9	32	32	0	27
MANCHESTER UNITED	25	10	7	8	36	42	-6	27
COVENTRY	26	10	7	9	33	43	-10	27
TOTTENHAM	27	9	9	9	29	43	-14	27
ASTON VILLA	23	7	11	5	28	21	7	25
IPSWICH	26	10	4	12	34	34	0	24
NORWICH	25	5	14	6	34	39	-5	24
MANCHESTER CITY	26	7	9	10	36	33	3	23
DERBY	25	8	6	11	29	44	-15	22
BOLTON	24	7	6	11	31	42	-11	20
WOLVES	26	8	3	15	25	46	-21	19
MIDDLESBROUGH	25	6	6	13	32	36	-4	18
QPR	26	4	10	12	24	38	-14	18
CHELSEA	26	4	6	16	29	56	-27	14
BIRMINGHAM	26	3	4	19	22	43	-21	10

AS AT 3 MARCH 1979

	P	W	D	L	F	A	GD	PTS
LIVERPOOL	26	19	4	3	58	10	48	42
EVERTON	28	14	10	4	39	24	15	38
WBA	25	15	6	4	52	25	27	36
ARSENAL	28	14	8	6	45	25	20	36
LEEDS	29	13	10	6	53	35	18	36
NOTTINGHAM FOREST	24	10	12	2	28	16	12	32
MANCHESTER UNITED	27	12	7	8	40	43	-3	31
SOUTHAMPTON	28	10	9	9	34	32	2	29
TOTTENHAM	28	10	9	9	31	43	-12	29
BRISTOL CITY	30	10	8	12	35	37	-2	28
ASTON VILLA	24	8	11	5	29	21	8	27
IPSWICH	28	11	5	12	36	35	1	27
COVENTRY	27	10	7	10	34	46	-12	27
MANCHESTER CITY	28	8	10	10	40	36	4	26
NORWICH	27	5	16	6	38	43	-5	26
DERBY	27	8	6	13	29	47	-18	22
MIDDLESBROUGH	26	7	6	13	35	37	-2	20
BOLTON	25	7	6	12	32	44	-12	20
WOLVES	27	8	3	16	26	49	-23	19
QPR	28	4	10	14	25	42	-17	18
CHELSEA	27	4	7	16	29	56	-27	15
BIRMINGHAM	27	3	4	20	22	44	-22	10

TUESDAY 27TH FEBRUARY 1979:

Manchester City 2   Norwich 2

WEDNESDAY 28TH FEBRUARY 1979:

Derby 0   Ipswich 1

Manchester United 2   QPR 0

SATURDAY 3RD MARCH 1979:

Aston Villa 1   Birmingham 0

Bristol City 1   Manchester United 2

Chelsea 0   Liverpool 0

Coventry 1   WBA 3

Everton 2   QPR 1

Ipswich 1   Nottingham Forest 1

Leeds 2   Norwich 2

Manchester City 2   Bolton 1

Southampton 2   Arsenal 0

Tottenham 2   Derby 0

Wolves 1   Middlesbrough 3

AS AT 10 MARCH 1979

	P	W	D	L	F	A	GD	PTS
LIVERPOOL	27	19	5	3	58	10	48	43
EVERTON	30	15	11	4	42	26	16	41
ARSENAL	29	15	8	6	47	25	22	38
LEEDS	30	14	10	6	54	35	19	38
WBA	25	15	6	4	52	25	27	36
NOTTINGHAM FOREST	25	10	13	2	29	17	12	33
MANCHESTER UNITED	27	12	7	8	40	43	-3	31
ASTON VILLA	26	9	11	6	32	23	9	29
SOUTHAMPTON	28	10	9	9	34	32	2	29
NORWICH	29	6	17	6	40	43	-3	29
TOTTENHAM	28	10	9	9	31	43	-12	29
COVENTRY	29	10	9	10	34	46	-12	29
BRISTOL CITY	31	10	8	13	35	39	-4	28
IPSWICH	28	11	5	12	36	35	1	27
MANCHESTER CITY	28	8	10	10	40	36	4	26
MIDDLESBROUGH	28	8	6	14	38	39	-1	22
DERBY	28	8	6	14	29	48	-19	22
BOLTON	26	7	6	13	32	47	-15	20
WOLVES	28	8	4	16	26	49	-23	20
QPR	29	4	10	15	26	45	-19	18
CHELSEA	28	4	7	17	29	58	-29	15
BIRMINGHAM	29	4	5	20	25	45	-20	13

TUESDAY 6TH MARCH 1979:

Birmingham 3	QPR 1
Coventry 0	Liverpool 0
Middlesbrough 1	Everton 2

WEDNESDAY 7TH MARCH 1979:

Aston Villa 3	Bolton 0
Norwich 0	Wolves 0

SATURDAY 10TH MARCH 1979:

Arsenal 2	Bristol City 0
Birmingham 0	Coventry 0
Derby 0	Leeds 1
Everton 1	Nottingham Forest 1
Middlesbrough 2	Aston Villa 0
Norwich 2	Chelsea 0

AS AT 17 MARCH 1979

	P	W	D	L	F	A	GD	PTS
LIVERPOOL	28	19	6	3	59	11	48	44
EVERTON	31	15	12	4	43	27	16	42
WBA	26	16	6	4	53	25	28	38
ARSENAL	30	15	8	7	47	27	20	38
LEEDS	30	14	10	6	54	35	19	38
NOTTINGHAM FOREST	26	11	13	2	31	18	13	35
MANCHESTER UNITED	27	12	7	8	40	43	-3	31
COVENTRY	31	10	11	10	37	49	-12	31
IPSWICH	30	12	6	12	39	36	3	30
NORWICH	31	6	18	7	41	45	-4	30
TOTTENHAM	29	10	10	9	31	43	-12	30
ASTON VILLA	26	9	11	6	32	23	9	29
SOUTHAMPTON	28	10	9	9	34	32	2	29
BRISTOL CITY	32	10	9	13	36	40	-4	29
MANCHESTER CITY	28	8	10	10	40	36	4	26
MIDDLESBROUGH	30	9	7	14	42	41	1	25
DERBY	29	8	6	15	30	51	-21	22
BOLTON	27	7	7	13	34	49	-15	21
QPR	30	5	10	15	29	46	-17	20
WOLVES	28	8	4	16	26	49	-23	20
CHELSEA	30	4	7	19	30	62	-32	15
BIRMINGHAM	29	4	5	20	25	45	-20	13

TUESDAY 13TH MARCH 1979:

Ipswich 1 — Coventry 1
Liverpool 1 — Everton 1
Middlesbrough 3 — Derby 1

WEDNESDAY 14TH MARCH 1979:

Nottingham Forest 2 — Norwich 1
WBA 1 — Chelsea 0

SATURDAY 17TH MARCH 1979:

Bristol City 1 — Middlesbrough 1
Chelsea 1 — QPR 3
Coventry 2 — Bolton 2
Ipswich 2 — Arsenal 0
Tottenham 0 — Norwich 0

121

AS AT 24 MARCH 1979

	P	W	D	L	F	A	GD	PTS
LIVERPOOL	30	21	6	3	63	11	52	48
EVERTON	32	15	13	4	43	27	16	43
WBA	27	17	6	4	55	26	29	40
ARSENAL	31	15	9	7	48	28	20	39
LEEDS	31	14	10	7	55	39	16	38
NOTTINGHAM FOREST	27	12	13	2	34	18	16	37
MANCHESTER UNITED	29	13	7	9	47	48	-1	33
COVENTRY	33	11	11	11	41	55	-14	33
NORWICH	32	7	18	7	44	45	-1	32
TOTTENHAM	30	11	10	9	34	45	-11	32
ASTON VILLA	28	10	11	7	37	27	10	31
IPSWICH	31	12	6	13	39	38	1	30
SOUTHAMPTON	29	10	9	10	34	34	0	29
BRISTOL CITY	33	10	9	14	36	43	-7	29
MANCHESTER CITY	29	8	11	10	41	37	4	27
MIDDLESBROUGH	31	10	7	14	44	42	2	27
DERBY	31	9	7	15	33	51	-18	25
BOLTON	29	8	7	14	36	52	-16	23
WOLVES	30	9	4	17	28	52	-24	22
QPR	32	5	10	17	31	51	-20	20
CHELSEA	31	4	7	20	31	64	-33	15
BIRMINGHAM	30	4	5	21	26	47	-21	13

TUESDAY 20TH MARCH 1979:

Aston Villa 3	QPR 1
Coventry 4	Manchester United 3
Liverpool 2	Wolves 0

WEDNESDAY 21ST MARCH 1979:

Derby 3	Bolton 0

SATURDAY 24TH MARCH 1979:

Arsenal 1	Manchester City 1
Aston Villa 2	Tottenham 3
Bolton 2	Southampton 0
Chelsea 1	Wolves 2
Derby 0	Everton 2
Liverpool 2	Ipswich 0
Manchester United 4	Leeds 1
Middlesbrough 2	Birmingham 1
Norwich 3	Bristol City 0
Nottingham Forest 3	Coventry 0
WBA 2	QPR 1

AS AT 30 MARCH 1979

	P	W	D	L	F	A	GD	PTS
LIVERPOOL	30	21	6	3	63	11	52	48
EVERTON	33	15	14	4	45	29	16	44
WBA	28	18	6	4	57	27	30	42
NOTTINGHAM FOREST	28	13	13	2	40	18	22	39
ARSENAL	32	15	9	8	50	32	18	39
LEEDS	31	14	10	7	55	39	16	38
MANCHESTER UNITED	30	13	8	9	49	50	-1	38
COVENTRY	34	11	12	11	42	56	-14	34
NORWICH	34	7	19	8	46	48	-2	33
TOTTENHAM	31	11	11	9	34	45	-11	33
ASTON VILLA	29	10	12	7	38	28	10	32
IPSWICH	31	12	6	13	39	38	1	30
SOUTHAMPTON	30	10	10	10	34	34	0	30
BRISTOL CITY	33	10	9	14	36	43	-7	29
MANCHESTER CITY	30	8	12	10	42	38	4	28
MIDDLESBROUGH	32	10	8	14	46	44	2	28
BOLTON	30	9	7	14	40	54	-14	25
DERBY	32	9	7	16	34	53	-19	25
WOLVES	31	9	5	17	29	53	-24	23
QPR	32	5	10	17	31	51	-20	20
BIRMINGHAM	31	5	5	21	27	47	-20	15
CHELSEA	32	4	7	21	31	70	-39	15

MONDAY 26TH MARCH 1979:

Bolton 4	Arsenal 2
WBA 2	Derby 1

TUESDAY 27TH MARCH 1979:

Birmingham 1	Norwich 0
Middlesbrough 2	Manchester United 2
Wolves 1	Manchester City 1

WEDNESDAY 28TH MARCH 1979:

Aston Villa 1	Coventry 1
Nottingham Forest 6	Chelsea 0
Tottenham 0	Southampton 0

FRIDAY 30TH MARCH 1979:

Everton 2	Norwich 2

123

SATURDAY 31ST MARCH 1979:

Bristol City 2	Birmingham 1	
Ipswich 2	Manchester City 1	
Middlesbrough 1	Tottenham 0	
Nottingham Forest 1	Bolton 1	
QPR 2	Derby 2	
Southampton 2	Leeds 2	

AS AT 31 MARCH 1979

	P	W	D	L	F	A	GD	PTS
LIVERPOOL	30	21	6	3	63	11	52	48
EVERTON	33	15	14	4	45	29	16	44
WBA	28	18	6	4	57	27	30	42
NOTTINGHAM FOREST	29	13	14	2	41	19	22	40
ARSENAL	32	15	9	8	50	32	18	39
LEEDS	32	14	11	7	57	41	16	39
MANCHESTER UNITED	30	13	8	9	49	50	-1	34
COVENTRY	34	11	12	11	42	56	-14	34
NORWICH	34	7	19	8	46	48	-2	33
TOTTENHAM	32	11	11	10	34	46	-12	33
ASTON VILLA	29	10	12	7	38	28	10	32
IPSWICH	32	13	6	13	41	39	2	32
SOUTHAMPTON	31	10	11	10	36	36	0	31
BRISTOL CITY	34	11	9	14	38	44	-6	31
MIDDLESBROUGH	33	11	8	14	47	44	3	30
MANCHESTER CITY	31	8	12	11	43	40	3	28
BOLTON	31	9	8	14	41	55	-14	26
DERBY	33	9	8	16	36	55	-19	26
WOLVES	31	9	5	17	29	53	-24	23
QPR	33	5	11	17	33	53	-20	21
BIRMINGHAM	32	5	5	22	28	49	-21	15
CHELSEA	32	4	7	21	31	70	-39	15

TUESDAY 3RD APRIL 1979:

Arsenal 1	Coventry 1
Birmingham 1	Ipswich 1
Bolton 3	Everton 1
Bristol City 2	QPR 0
Wolves 3	Tottenham 2

WEDNESDAY 4TH APRIL 1979:

Chelsea 1	Derby 1
Nottingham Forest 4	Aston Villa 0
WBA 4	Manchester City 0

AS AT 4 APRIL 1979

	P	W	D	L	F	A	GD	PTS
LIVERPOOL	30	21	6	3	63	11	52	48
WBA	29	19	6	4	61	27	34	44
EVERTON	34	15	14	5	46	32	14	44
NOTTINGHAM FOREST	30	14	14	2	45	19	26	42
ARSENAL	33	15	10	8	51	33	18	40
LEEDS	32	14	11	7	57	41	16	39
COVENTRY	35	11	13	11	43	57	-14	35
MANCHESTER UNITED	30	13	8	9	49	50	-1	34
IPSWICH	33	13	7	13	42	40	2	33
NORWICH	34	7	19	8	46	48	-2	33
BRISTOL CITY	35	12	9	14	40	44	-4	33
TOTTENHAM	33	11	11	11	36	49	-13	33
ASTON VILLA	30	10	12	8	38	32	6	32
SOUTHAMPTON	31	10	11	10	36	36	0	31
MIDDLESBROUGH	33	11	8	14	47	44	3	30
MANCHESTER CITY	32	8	12	12	43	44	-1	28
BOLTON	32	10	8	14	44	56	-12	28
DERBY	34	9	9	16	37	56	-19	27
WOLVES	32	10	5	17	32	55	-23	25
QPR	34	5	11	18	33	55	-22	21
BIRMINGHAM	33	5	6	22	29	50	-21	16
CHELSEA	33	4	8	21	32	71	-39	16

125

SATURDAY 7TH APRIL 1979:

Birmingham 2	Southampton 2		
Bolton 2	QPR 1		
Chelsea 1	Nottingham Forest 3		
Coventry 1	Aston Villa 1		
Derby 0	Bristol City 1		
Leeds 1	Ipswich 1		
Liverpool 3	Arsenal 0		
Manchester City 3	Wolves 1		
Norwich 2	Manchester United 2		
Tottenham 1	Middlesbrough 2		
WBA 1	Everton 0		

AS AT 7 APRIL 1979

	P	W	D	L	F	A	GD	PTS
LIVERPOOL	31	22	6	3	66	11	55	50
WBA	30	20	6	4	62	27	35	46
NOTTINGHAM FOREST	31	15	14	2	48	20	28	44
EVERTON	35	15	14	6	46	33	13	44
LEEDS	33	14	12	7	58	42	16	40
ARSENAL	34	15	10	9	51	36	15	40
COVENTRY	36	11	14	11	44	58	-14	36
MANCHESTER UNITED	31	13	9	9	51	52	-1	35
BRISTOL CITY	36	13	9	14	41	44	-3	35
IPSWICH	34	13	8	13	43	41	2	34
NORWICH	35	7	20	8	48	50	-2	34
ASTON VILLA	31	10	13	8	39	33	6	33
TOTTENHAM	34	11	11	12	37	51	-14	33
MIDDLESBROUGH	34	12	8	14	49	45	4	32
SOUTHAMPTON	32	10	12	10	38	38	0	32
MANCHESTER CITY	33	9	12	12	46	45	1	30
BOLTON	33	11	8	14	46	57	-11	30
DERBY	35	9	9	17	37	57	-20	27
WOLVES	33	10	5	18	33	58	-25	25
QPR	35	5	11	19	34	57	-23	21
BIRMINGHAM	34	5	7	22	31	52	-21	17
CHELSEA	34	4	8	22	33	74	-41	16

AS AT 13 APRIL 1979

	P	W	D	L	F	A	GD	PTS
LIVERPOOL	32	23	6	3	67	11	56	52
WBA	31	20	7	4	63	28	35	47
EVERTON	36	15	15	6	49	36	13	45
NOTTINGHAM FOREST	31	15	14	2	48	20	28	44
ARSENAL	35	16	10	9	52	36	16	42
LEEDS	34	14	12	8	58	43	15	40
BRISTOL CITY	37	14	9	14	44	45	-1	37
COVENTRY	37	11	15	11	47	61	-14	37
MANCHESTER UNITED	32	13	9	10	52	54	-2	35
NORWICH	36	7	21	8	48	50	-2	35
ASTON VILLA	32	10	14	8	42	36	6	34
MIDDLESBROUGH	35	13	8	14	50	45	5	34
IPSWICH	34	13	8	13	43	41	2	34
SOUTHAMPTON	33	10	13	10	39	39	0	33
TOTTENHAM	35	11	11	13	37	52	-15	33
BOLTON	34	12	8	14	48	58	-10	32
MANCHESTER CITY	33	9	12	12	46	45	1	30
DERBY	36	9	10	17	40	60	-20	28
WOLVES	34	9	5	19	33	59	-26	25
QPR	36	5	12	19	34	57	-23	22
BIRMINGHAM	34	5	7	22	31	52	-21	17
CHELSEA	35	4	8	23	34	77	-43	16

TUESDAY 10TH APRIL 1979:

Arsenal 1 Tottenham 0

Bristol City 3 Chelsea 1

Everton 3 Coventry 3

Middlesbrough 1 Leeds 0

Wolves 0 Liverpool 1

WEDNESDAY 11TH APRIL 1979:

Aston Villa 3 Derby 3

Manchester United 1 Bolton 2

FRIDAY 13TH APRIL 1979:

QPR 0 Norwich 0

Southampton 1 WBA 1

127

SATURDAY 14TH APRIL 1979:

Birmingham 1	Wolves 1
Bolton 0	Middlesbrough 0
Chelsea 1	Southampton 2
Coventry 3	Bristol City 2
Derby 1	Nottingham Forest 2
Leeds 1	Aston Villa 0
Liverpool 2	Manchester United 0
Manchester City 0	Everton 0
Norwich 0	Ipswich 1
Tottenham 1	QPR 1
WBA 1	Arsenal 1

AS AT 14 APRIL 1979

	P	W	D	L	F	A	GD	PTS
LIVERPOOL	33	24	6	3	69	11	58	54
WBA	32	20	8	4	64	29	35	48
NOTTINGHAM FOREST	32	16	14	2	50	21	29	46
EVERTON	37	15	16	6	49	36	13	46
ARSENAL	36	16	11	9	53	37	16	43
LEEDS	35	15	12	8	59	43	16	42
COVENTRY	38	12	15	11	50	63	-13	39
BRISTOL CITY	38	14	9	15	46	48	-2	37
IPSWICH	35	14	8	13	44	41	3	36
MIDDLESBROUGH	36	13	9	14	50	45	5	35
SOUTHAMPTON	34	11	13	10	41	40	1	35
NORWICH	37	7	21	9	48	51	-3	35
MANCHESTER UNITED	33	13	9	11	52	56	-4	35
ASTON VILLA	33	10	14	9	42	37	5	34
TOTTENHAM	36	11	12	13	38	53	-15	34
BOLTON	35	12	9	14	48	58	-10	33
MANCHESTER CITY	34	9	13	12	46	45	1	31
DERBY	37	9	10	18	41	62	-21	28
WOLVES	35	10	6	19	34	60	-26	26
QPR	37	5	13	19	35	58	-23	23
BIRMINGHAM	35	5	8	22	32	53	-21	18
CHELSEA	36	4	8	24	35	79	-44	16

MONDAY 16TH APRIL 1979:

Arsenal 5	Chelsea 2
Aston Villa 3	Liverpool 1
Everton 1	Bolton 0
Ipswich 2	Derby 1
Manchester United 0	Coventry 0
Nottingham Forest 0	Leeds 0
Southampton 3	Tottenham 3
Wolves 1	Norwich 0

AS AT 16 APRIL 1979

	P	W	D	L	F	A	GD	PTS
LIVERPOOL	34	24	6	4	70	14	56	54
WBA	32	20	8	4	64	29	35	48
EVERTON	38	16	16	6	50	36	14	48
NOTTINGHAM FOREST	33	16	15	2	50	21	29	47
ARSENAL	37	17	11	9	58	39	19	45
LEEDS	36	15	13	8	59	43	16	43
COVENTRY	39	12	16	11	50	63	-13	40
IPSWICH	36	15	8	13	46	42	4	38
BRISTOL CITY	38	14	9	15	46	48	-2	37
ASTON VILLA	34	11	14	9	45	38	7	36
SOUTHAMPTON	35	11	14	10	44	43	1	36
MANCHESTER UNITED	34	13	10	11	52	56	-4	36
MIDDLESBROUGH	36	13	9	14	50	45	5	35
NORWICH	38	7	21	10	48	52	-4	35
TOTTENHAM	37	11	13	13	41	56	-15	35
BOLTON	36	12	9	15	48	59	-11	33
MANCHESTER CITY	34	9	13	12	46	45	1	31
DERBY	38	9	10	19	42	64	-22	28
WOLVES	36	11	6	19	35	60	-25	28
QPR	37	5	13	19	35	58	-23	23
BIRMINGHAM	35	5	8	22	32	53	-21	18
CHELSEA	37	4	8	25	37	84	-47	16

TUESDAY 17TH APRIL 1979:

Bristol City 1	WBA 0
Ipswich 3	Birmingham 0
Middlesbrough 2	Manchester City 0

WEDNESDAY 18TH APRIL 1979:

Nottingham Forest 1	Manchester United 1

AS AT 18 APRIL 1979

	P	W	D	L	F	A	GD	PTS
LIVERPOOL	34	24	6	4	70	14	56	54
WBA	33	20	8	5	64	30	34	48
NOTTINGHAM FOREST	34	16	16	2	51	22	29	48
EVERTON	38	16	16	6	50	36	14	48
ARSENAL	37	17	11	9	58	39	19	45
LEEDS	36	15	13	8	59	43	16	43
IPSWICH	37	16	8	13	49	42	7	40
COVENTRY	39	12	16	11	50	63	-13	40
BRISTOL CITY	39	15	9	15	47	48	-1	39
MIDDLESBROUGH	37	14	9	14	52	45	7	37
MANCHESTER UNITED	35	13	11	11	53	57	-4	37
ASTON VILLA	34	11	14	9	45	38	7	36
SOUTHAMPTON	35	11	14	10	44	43	1	36
NORWICH	38	7	21	10	48	52	-4	35
TOTTENHAM	37	11	13	13	41	56	-15	35
BOLTON	36	12	9	15	48	59	-11	33
MANCHESTER CITY	35	9	13	13	46	47	-1	31
DERBY	38	9	10	19	42	64	-22	28
WOLVES	36	11	6	19	35	60	-25	28
QPR	37	5	13	19	35	58	-23	23
BIRMINGHAM	36	5	8	23	32	56	-24	18
CHELSEA	37	4	8	25	37	84	-47	16

AS AT 21 APRIL 1979

	P	W	D	L	F	A	GD	PTS
LIVERPOOL	35	25	6	4	71	14	57	56
NOTTINGHAM FOREST	35	17	16	2	53	22	31	50
WBA	34	20	9	5	65	31	34	49
EVERTON	39	16	16	7	50	37	13	48
ARSENAL	38	17	11	10	58	41	17	45
LEEDS	37	16	13	8	60	43	17	45
IPSWICH	38	17	8	13	52	44	8	42
COVENTRY	40	13	16	11	54	63	-9	42
BRISTOL CITY	40	15	9	16	47	49	-2	39
ASTON VILLA	35	12	14	9	47	39	8	38
MANCHESTER UNITED	36	13	12	11	54	58	-4	38
MIDDLESBROUGH	38	14	9	15	53	47	6	37
SOUTHAMPTON	36	11	14	11	44	47	-3	36
TOTTENHAM	38	11	14	13	42	57	-15	36
NORWICH	39	7	21	11	49	54	-5	35
MANCHESTER CITY	36	10	13	13	49	48	1	33
BOLTON	37	12	9	16	50	62	-12	33
DERBY	39	10	10	19	44	64	-20	30
WOLVES	37	11	7	19	36	61	-25	29
QPR	38	5	13	20	36	61	-25	23
BIRMINGHAM	37	5	8	24	32	58	-26	18
CHELSEA	38	5	8	25	39	85	-46	18

131

SATURDAY 21ST APRIL 1979:

Birmingham 0	Nottingham Forest 2
Bolton 2	Ipswich 3
Chelsea 2	Middlesbrough 1
Coventry 4	Southampton 0
Derby 2	Arsenal 0
Leeds 1	Everton 0
Liverpool 1	Bristol City 0
Manchester City 3	QPR 1
Norwich 1	Aston Villa 2
Tottenham 1	Manchester United 1
WBA 1	Wolves 1

TUESDAY 24TH APRIL 1979:

Birmingham 1	WBA 1	
Manchester City 1	Middlesbrough 0	
Southampton 1	Liverpool 1	
Wolves 4	Derby 0	

WEDNESDAY 25TH APRIL 1979:

Aston Villa 5	Arsenal 1
Leeds 5	Bolton 1
Manchester United 1	Norwich 0

AS AT 25 APRIL 1979

	P	W	D	L	F	A	GD	PTS
LIVERPOOL	36	25	7	4	72	15	57	57
WBA	35	20	10	5	66	32	34	50
NOTTINGHAM FOREST	35	17	16	2	53	22	31	50
EVERTON	39	16	16	7	50	37	13	48
LEEDS	38	17	13	8	65	44	21	47
ARSENAL	39	17	11	11	59	46	13	45
IPSWICH	38	17	8	13	52	44	8	42
COVENTRY	40	13	16	11	54	63	-9	42
ASTON VILLA	36	13	14	9	52	40	12	40
MANCHESTER UNITED	37	14	12	11	55	58	-3	40
BRISTOL CITY	40	15	9	16	47	49	-2	39
MIDDLESBROUGH	39	14	9	16	53	48	5	37
SOUTHAMPTON	37	11	15	11	45	48	-3	37
TOTTENHAM	38	11	14	13	42	57	-15	36
MANCHESTER CITY	37	11	13	13	50	48	2	35
NORWICH	40	7	21	12	49	55	-6	35
BOLTON	38	12	9	17	51	67	-16	33
WOLVES	38	12	7	19	40	61	-21	31
DERBY	40	10	10	20	44	68	-24	30
QPR	38	5	13	20	36	61	-25	23
BIRMINGHAM	38	5	9	24	33	59	-26	19
CHELSEA	38	5	8	25	39	85	-46	18

SATURDAY 28TH APRIL 1979:

Arsenal 1	Norwich 1
Aston Villa 2	Chelsea 1
Bristol City 0	Leeds 0
Everton 1	Birmingham c
Ipswich 2	Tottenham 1
Manchester United 0	Derby 0
Middlesbrough 1	WBA 1
Nottingham Forest 0	Liverpool 0
QPR 5	Coventry 1
Southampton 1	Manchester C ty 0
Wolves 1	Bolton 1

AS AT 28 APRIL 1979

	P	W	D	L	F	A	GD	PTS
LIVERPOOL	37	25	8	4	72	15	57	58
WBA	36	20	11	5	67	33	34	51
NOTTINGHAM FOREST	36	17	17	2	53	22	31	51
EVERTON	40	17	16	7	51	37	14	50
LEEDS	39	17	14	8	65	44	21	48
ARSENAL	40	17	12	11	60	47	13	46
IPSWICH	39	18	8	13	54	45	9	44
ASTON VILLA	37	14	14	9	54	41	13	42
COVENTRY	41	13	16	12	55	68	-13	42
MANCHESTER UNITED	38	14	13	11	55	58	-3	41
BRISTOL CITY	41	15	10	16	47	49	-2	40
SOUTHAMPTON	38	12	15	11	46	48	-2	39
MIDDLESBROUGH	40	14	10	16	54	49	5	38
NORWICH	41	7	22	12	50	56	-6	36
TOTTENHAM	39	11	14	14	43	59	-16	36
MANCHESTER CITY	38	11	13	14	50	49	1	35
BOLTON	39	12	10	17	52	68	-16	34
WOLVES	39	12	8	19	41	62	-21	32
DERBY	41	10	11	20	44	68	-24	31
QPR	39	6	13	20	41	62	-21	25
BIRMINGHAM	39	5	9	25	33	60	-27	19
CHELSEA	39	5	8	26	40	87	-47	18

AS AT 2 MAY 1979

	P	W	D	L	F	A	GD	PTS
LIVERPOOL	38	26	8	4	76	16	60	60
WBA	37	21	11	5	69	33	36	53
NOTTINGHAM FOREST	38	18	17	3	54	23	31	53
EVERTON	41	17	16	8	51	39	12	50
LEEDS	39	17	14	8	65	44	21	48
ARSENAL	40	17	12	11	60	47	13	46
IPSWICH	40	18	9	13	56	47	9	45
ASTON VILLA	38	14	15	9	56	43	13	43
MANCHESTER UNITED	39	14	14	11	56	59	-3	42
COVENTRY	41	13	16	12	55	68	-13	42
BRISTOL CITY	41	15	10	16	47	49	-2	40
SOUTHAMPTON	40	12	16	12	47	50	-3	40
MIDDLESBROUGH	40	14	10	16	54	49	5	38
MANCHESTER CITY	39	12	13	14	53	50	3	37
NORWICH	41	7	22	12	50	56	-6	36
TOTTENHAM	39	11	14	14	43	59	-16	36
BOLTON	40	12	10	18	53	72	-19	34
WOLVES	40	13	8	19	42	62	-20	34
DERBY	41	10	11	20	44	68	-24	31
QPR	39	6	13	20	41	62	-21	25
BIRMINGHAM	40	5	9	26	34	63	-29	19
CHELSEA	39	5	8	26	40	87	-47	18

134

MONDAY 30TH APRIL 1979:

Southampton 1   Manchester United 1

Wolves 1   Nottingham Forest 0

TUESDAY 1ST MAY 1979:

Bolton 1   Liverpool 4

Everton 0   WBA 2

Manchester City 3   Birmingham 1

WEDNESDAY 2ND MAY 1979:

Aston Villa 2   Ipswich 2

Nottingham Forest 1   Southampton 0

AS AT 5 MAY 1979

	P	W	D	L	F	A	GD	PTS
LIVERPOOL	39	27	8	4	78	16	62	62
WBA	38	22	11	5	70	33	37	55
NOTTINGHAM FOREST	39	18	18	3	55	24	31	54
EVERTON	42	17	17	8	52	40	12	51
LEEDS	40	18	14	8	69	47	22	50
ARSENAL	41	17	13	11	60	47	13	47
IPSWICH	41	19	9	13	59	49	10	47
ASTON VILLA	39	14	16	9	56	43	13	44
COVENTRY	42	14	16	12	58	68	-10	44
MANCHESTER UNITED	40	14	14	12	56	60	-4	42
MIDDLESBROUGH	41	15	10	16	57	49	8	40
BRISTOL CITY	42	15	10	17	47	51	-4	40
SOUTHAMPTON	41	12	16	13	47	52	-5	40
MANCHESTER CITY	40	13	13	14	55	50	5	39
NORWICH	42	7	23	12	51	57	-6	37
TOTTENHAM	40	11	15	14	44	60	-16	37
BOLTON	41	12	11	18	53	72	-19	35
WOLVES	41	13	8	20	42	65	-23	34
DERBY	42	10	11	21	44	71	-27	31
QPR	40	6	13	21	44	66	-22	25
BIRMINGHAM	41	5	10	26	34	63	-29	20
CHELSEA	40	5	8	27	42	90	-48	18

FRIDAY 4TH MAY 1979:

Leeds 4   QPR 3

SATURDAY 5TH MAY 1979:

Birmingham 0   Arsenal 0

Bolton 0   Aston Villa 0

Chelsea 2   Ipswich 3

Coventry 3   Wolves 0

Derby 0   Middlesbrough 3

Liverpool 2   Southampton 0

Manchester City 2   Bristol City 0

Norwich 1   Nottingham Forest 1

Tottenham 1   Everton 1

WBA 1   Manchester United 0

AS AT 11 MAY 1979

	P	W	D	L	F	A	GD	PTS
LIVERPOOL	41	29	8	4	82	16	66	66
WBA	40	24	11	5	72	33	39	59
NOTTINGHAM FOREST	40	19	18	3	58	25	33	56
EVERTON	42	17	17	8	52	40	12	51
LEEDS	40	18	14	8	69	47	22	50
IPSWICH	42	20	9	13	63	49	14	49
ARSENAL	41	17	13	11	60	47	13	47
ASTON VILLA	41	14	16	11	56	47	9	44
MANCHESTER UNITED	41	15	14	12	59	62	-3	44
COVENTRY	42	14	16	12	58	68	-10	44
MIDDLESBROUGH	42	15	10	17	57	50	7	40
BRISTOL CITY	42	15	10	17	47	51	-4	40
SOUTHAMPTON	42	12	16	14	47	53	-6	40
MANCHESTER CITY	41	13	13	15	56	53	3	39
TOTTENHAM	41	12	15	14	47	61	-14	39
NORWICH	42	7	23	12	51	57	-6	37
BOLTON	42	12	11	19	54	75	-21	35
WOLVES	42	13	8	21	44	68	-24	34
DERBY	42	10	11	21	44	71	-27	31
QPR	42	6	13	23	45	73	-28	25
BIRMINGHAM	42	6	10	26	37	64	-27	22
CHELSEA	40	5	8	27	42	90	-48	18

136

MONDAY 7TH MAY 1979:

Manchester United 3 — Wolves 2

QPR 1 — Birmingham 3

TUESDAY 8TH MAY 1979:

Bolton 1 — Tottenham 3

Liverpool 3 — Aston Villa 0

WBA 1 — Southampton 0

WEDNESDAY 9TH MAY 1979:

Nottingham Forest 3 — Manchester City 1

FRIDAY 11TH MAY 1979:

Aston Villa 0 — WBA 1

Middlesbrough 0 — Liverpool 1

QPR 0 — Ipswich 4

AS AT 18 MAY 1979

	P	W	D	L	F	A	GD	PTS
LIVERPOOL	42	30	8	4	85	16	69	68
NOTTINGHAM FOREST	42	21	18	3	61	26	35	60
WBA	42	24	11	7	72	35	37	59
EVERTON	42	17	17	8	52	40	12	51
LEEDS	42	18	14	10	70	52	18	50
IPSWICH	42	20	9	13	63	49	14	49
ARSENAL	42	17	14	11	61	48	13	48
ASTON VILLA	42	15	16	11	59	49	10	46
MANCHESTER UNITED	42	15	15	12	60	63	-3	45
COVENTRY	42	14	16	12	58	68	-10	44
TOTTENHAM	42	13	15	14	48	61	-13	41
MIDDLESBROUGH	42	15	10	17	57	50	7	40
BRISTOL CITY	42	15	10	17	47	51	-4	40
SOUTHAMPTON	42	12	16	14	47	53	-6	40
MANCHESTER CITY	42	13	13	16	58	56	2	39
NORWICH	42	7	23	12	51	57	-6	37
BOLTON	42	12	11	19	54	75	-21	35
WOLVES	42	13	8	21	44	68	-24	34
DERBY	42	10	11	21	44	71	-27	31
QPR	42	6	13	23	45	73	-28	25
BIRMINGHAM	42	6	10	26	37	64	-27	22
CHELSEA	42	5	10	27	44	92	-48	20

137

MONDAY 14TH MAY 1979:

Chelsea 1 Arsenal 1

Tottenham 1 WBA 0

TUESDAY 15TH MAY 1979:

Leeds 1 Nottingham Forest 2

Manchester City 2 Aston Villa 3

WEDNESDAY 16TH MAY 1979:

Manchester United 1 Chelsea 1

THURSDAY 17TH MAY 1979:

Leeds 0 Liverpool 3

FRIDAY 18TH MAY 1979:

WBA 0 Nottingham Forest 1